BILL SEVERN'S
MAGIC IN MIND

BILL SEVERN'S MAGIC IN MIND

Mystifying Mental Tricks

BILL SEVERN

Illustrated by Katherine Wood

STACKPOLE BOOKS

Published by
STACKPOLE BOOKS
Cameron and Kelker Streets
P.O. Box 1831
Harrisburg, PA 17105

Printed in the United States of America

First Paperback Edition 1993

10 9 8 7 6 5 4 3 2 1

Cover design by Caroline Miller

Library of Congress Cataloging-in-Publication Data

Severn, Bill.
    [Magic in mind]
    Bill Severn's magic in mind : mystifying mental tricks / Bill Severn.
      p.   cm.
    Originally published: New York : H.Z. Walck, 1974.
    ISBN 0-8117-2531-6
    1. Conjuring. 2. Telepathy. I. Title. II. Title: Magic in mind.
GV1553.S48   1993   92-20478
793.8—dc20   CIP

Contents

BILL SEVERN'S
MAGIC IN MIND

1

The Mental Magician

The magician who pulls a rabbit from a hat deceives the eye. But the mental magician deceives the mind. He creates the illusion that he is able to read minds, that he can transfer thoughts from his mind to the minds of others, can predict future happenings, and can perform other demonstrations of psychic phenomena.

What he does is no part of the serious scientific and psychological research into such things. Whether performing for a few friends or for a larger audience, he is an actor playing the role of a mentalist, an entertainer presenting a rehearsed show of mental magic. It is a form of theatrical make-believe that audiences have enjoyed since the beginnings of theater itself and is part of the fun thousands of amateurs have found in the hobby of performing magic.

The mental magician doesn't say it is all a trick, any more than the magician who takes a rabbit from a hat would break into a performance to explain that there is no real magic in what he does. He claims no supernormal powers, but he

3

suggests the possibility that they may exist for some people, demonstrates what might be accomplished if someone did possess such powers—and leaves it to the audience to decide how it is done.

Unlike the magician who displays his skill at deception, the mentalist avoids the appearance of trickery. He presents no visual magic show. His illusions are with thoughts, not with things.

He depends more on showmanship, personality, and acting ability than on the mechanics of what he does or the props he uses. If he is convincing, the audience centers its attention entirely on him and is not concerned with the apparently ordinary pads of paper, pencils, cards, envelopes, and other incidental things he has or the way in which he handles them. He *seems* to do it all with his mind.

The basic secrets

Most of the secrets of mental magic are simple ones, far simpler than the audience imagines. Some of the props are tricked, of course, but seldom in any elaborate manner. The mentalist relies more on subtlety than on apparatus. Because everything must be made to look as innocent as possible, the less there is to hide the better. Simple, bold, direct methods allow him to concentrate on the presentation, and that is what counts—not the trick as a magical puzzle designed to fool the spectators, but the illusion he can build around it in their minds, the effect that he can create of some psychic happening.

He has an advantage over other magicians in that his props can be carried in his pockets or in a briefcase. There are no suitcases filled with equipment, no boxes, tubes, and other bulky devices to set up and repack afterward. Most of his routines, no matter how small the things used in them, can be adapted for presentation to audiences of any size, almost anywhere.

Another advantage is that his audiences are often in a less challenging mood than they are when they watch an ordinary magic show. People know the usual magician is a trickster and they watch for every clue to his tricks with a fool-me-if-you-can attitude. But the mental magician presents no visible tricks as such, no obvious display of sleight of hand. The audience may guess that what he does is a trick and yet be less certain that it is, more willing to suspend disbelief, to go along with the illusion that he creates.

Everything he presents is an experiment, a test or an attempt, never with results guaranteed in advance. If he fails, he can always say that that particular experiment didn't work, that he just couldn't "get the thought clearly." As a mentalist, he is not expected to be right all the time. In fact, he may deliberately make minor mistakes, just to be more convincing.

Of course, if he is caught, even once, doing something tricky with his props, then the whole illusion of mental magic is gone as far as that audience is concerned. As simple as a trick may seem when reduced to its bare bones, the mechanics of it must be practiced until it can be done surely every time, naturally and almost automatically.

The mental magician must also avoid the *suggestion* of trickery in his handling of things and in what he says. He doesn't make a finger-waving exhibition of showing that his hands are empty; he merely lets it be seen that they are. He doesn't elaborately display a pocket handkerchief on both sides as a magician might before covering a glass with it; he simply takes it from his pocket, shakes it out, and drops it over the glass. He makes no attempt to "prove" that things are "ordinary and unprepared." It will be assumed that they are, unless he arouses suspicion by suggesting otherwise.

Many mentalists avoid the use of playing cards, or even manufactured alphabet and number cards, because they call to mind the card-manipulating magician. Some also contend that mental magic and other kinds of magic should never be mixed in the same program. On the other hand, there are any number of successful magicians who have included mental effects in their magic shows, and quite a few mentalists who combine both. It is something each performer must decide for himself.

Visibility and dramatic effect

One thing the ordinary magic show has that the mental magic show greatly lacks is visible entertainment, something for the audience to see. That is a disadvantage the mentalist must try to overcome. He must create a sense of something always happening, keep things moving, dramatize his effects, and build each routine to a climax to maintain the interest of the audience.

For the most part the audience can participate only indirectly, through a few spectators chosen to join in the experiments as representatives of the whole audience. The others can't see for themselves what is printed on the selected page of a book, for instance, or what may be written on a small slip of paper. They are asked to accept what happens on the basis of what a few spectators say is happening.

Whenever possible, the spectators who do take part in an experiment should be asked to read things aloud. Large cards or slates may also be used so things can be written for everyone to see and to give the entire audience something to watch. The plots of mental effects should be easy to follow, and the mentalist should make sure that the whole audience does understand exactly what is happening, or at least what he wants them to *think* is happening.

Setting the stage

The effects in this book are for solo performance. That is, the mentalist works alone, without seen or unseen assistants, confederates, or stooges, but rather with spectators chosen from the audience to take part.

When the audience is small, the performer can invite spectators to join in various experiments as he goes along, or he can go to where they are seated. But in a large room, or when he is working from a platform, he may want to select a "committee" of half a dozen spectators at the start. The group can be seated in chairs at the front, so he doesn't have to leave the platform or delay the performance to bring spectators up individually.

He will need a table, such as a card table or whatever other small table may be available, and if he is presenting more than one or two effects, he probably also will need an attaché case or briefcase to carry things in. But equipment generally should be kept to a minimum, since the whole idea is to suggest that what he does is with his mind alone.

The mentalist usually will position his table so that he can stand at the front of a room, with no spectators seated behind him. But he can't fuss over such arrangements. If he does happen to find himself surrounded by an audience, he may have to eliminate some routines from that particular program rather than risk exposing his secrets.

Dealing with spectators

When he gives any instructions to spectators, he must make sure that they understand exactly what he wants them to do. He should show them, if possible, and repeat the instructions if necessary. But their help should always be politely requested, never commanded, and if something goes wrong, no spectator should be openly criticized for it.

The mental magician's attitude should never be one of challenging the audience in a boastful or superior manner, and he should avoid being drawn into arguments or debates. Even if the performer can prove that he is right, he is not there to prove anything—only to entertain by offering in a modest and friendly way to "attempt" some interesting experiments that he wants to share with the audience, with their help and just for fun.

Practice and rehearsal

Aside from the necessary practice to learn the working of a trick, each effect should be carefully rehearsed, just as an actor would rehearse his part in a play. All the props should be set up and the words and movements acted out before an imagined audience. The mentalist should know exactly how the smallest thing will be picked up, displayed, handled, what will be in which pocket or in a certain position on the table, and where he will put it when he has finished using it. More than that, he should try to imagine what could go wrong and to plan in advance how he would handle the situation.

Planning the show

When the chosen effects have been individually practiced and rehearsed, they will have to be put together in a planned program, balanced and with good variety. The performer probably will want to start his show with something quick, direct, and impressive that requires very little buildup or handling of things by members of the audience. Each effect after that should be like one act in a play, with its own climax, but building in interest from one to the next, with what he considers his best effect to end the show.

Which effects he selects and how many he includes will depend in part on where he intends to perform and on the size and kind of audience. If he is going to entertain a small group of friends, two or three effects that use things he can carry in his pocket should be enough. For a larger audience, he will want to include props that are more visible from a distance, and perhaps four or five effects. He should know from rehearsal how long each effect will take to do, and allow for the time it will take spectators to handle things and carry out instructions.

He may find, when he puts a show together, that the props for one effect fill a pocket and leave no room in it for the things required for the next effect. In that case, he will have to rearrange the setup, decide which things are most essential to have in that particular pocket, and perhaps have the others in order in his briefcase or on the table.

Whatever show he gives, even if only for a few friends in his own living room, it should be planned and rehearsed. It is only from such rehearsals that he can gain the assurance and confidence he needs when he performs. And rehearsing tricks, trying them in various ways to achieve the best possible effect, is a good part of the fun of doing magic.

Experience and personality

Of course, no amount of rehearsal will replace the trial and error of actual performance before a real audience. It is only by giving shows, trying things, testing the audience reaction to them, that a performer learns what should be left out, what needs to be added, and how to point up each routine with words and actions to get the most from it in terms of impact and entertainment.

All the directions given in this book for what to say and do should be considered as suggestions, to be followed only to the extent that they may fit the performer's own style. He will want to find his own best ways of presentation, and he should translate the patter into his own words. Above all else, he should be himself in his role as mental magician. What he has to put across is not the tricks, but the convincing illusion he can create with them out of his own personality.

2

Extrasensory Deceptions

Symbolic Sight

How it looks:

"The standard symbols for scientific testing of extrasensory perception are a circle, a cross, three wavy lines, a square, and a star," you say. "I have printed those symbols on these office file cards." You show each of the symbols and then hand all the cards to a spectator and turn your back.

"Mix them, please," you tell him, "and when you're satisfied that they are thoroughly mixed, spread them all out face-down on the table so it will be impossible for me to see what is on them. Then just take any one—look at it and hold it with its face against your forehead while you think of that symbol."

You turn around and face him. After some effort, you announce which symbol he has in mind, and ask him to hold up the card and show it to everybody. Then you tell him:

11

"Please put it back with the others and mix them on the table again. This time, while my back is turned, take three—any three you wish. Look at them, hold them against your chest, and then turn your own back to me."

When he says he has done that, you face the spectators while he stands with his back toward you. Again, you concentrate, and then say: "One of the symbols you have is the star (or whatever it may be). . . . Will you hold it up, please—and then the cross that you have—and the square?"

For a final ESP experiment, while your back is turned again, you have him mix the symbols and spread them facedown on the table as before. You turn around, go to the table, take a red pen from your pocket, and draw a symbol on the back of each facedown card. Then you hold them up, one at a time, to show that your drawings match the hidden symbols on the faces of all five.

What you need:

Five office index file cards, the standard kind with printed lines on one side and the opposite side blank. These come in various sizes. Small 3-by-5-inch cards, which are easy to carry in the pocket, may be used for closeup performance. For a larger group, 4-by-8-inch cards should be used, with bigger symbols drawn on them.

A black marking pen and a red marking pen.

A typewriter eraser.

The secret and setup:

This routine is strong, direct, and can be presented almost anywhere. Its secret depends on the use of the file cards. The fact that they are manufactured with lines printed on what will be used as the backs allows for marking them in a way that can be seen from a fair distance. The performer quickly knows, from the back of a card, which symbol is on the face of it.

First, for those unfamiliar with the standard ESP symbols, a coding system that is often used by mentalists should be learned. It is an easy one to remember. The circle is one continuous line, so it is thought of as 1; the cross or plus sign is made with two lines, so it is thought of as 2; the three wavy vertical lines are 3; the four-sided square is 4; the five-pointed star is 5. Memorize them in that order and always think of them that way: circle, cross, lines, square, star — 1, 2, 3, 4, 5. Thus, if you see a mark that indicates "1" it is the circle card, "3" is the wavy-lines card, and so on.

The lined sides of index cards are manufactured with a *red* line at the top and *blue* lines spaced down the rest of the card. The red line will be your key. No matter in what position a card is held or placed on the table, you will look first for the red line, then for the blue lines, to count them mentally from the red-line starting point.

Put one of the cards on a table with the *red* line at the top. Make sure the typewriter eraser is clean and erase a full inch from each end of the *first* blue line beneath the red one. Erase it thoroughly, so no trace of the printed line remains at the ends.

Turn the card over so the blank face is up and so the narrow edges of the card are now at the top and bottom. With the black marking pen, draw a circle as large as will fit on the card.

Put that card aside and take another. Erase an inch from both ends of the *second* blue line beneath the red one, then turn it over and draw the cross vertically on the face of that

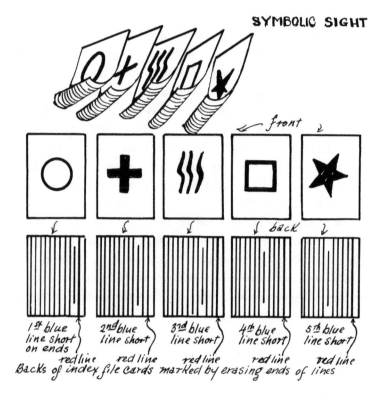

SYMBOLIC SIGHT

front

back

1st blue line short on ends | 2nd blue line short | 3rd blue line short | 4th blue line short | 5th blue line short

red line   red line   red line   red line   red line

Backs of index file cards marked by erasing ends of lines

card. From the back of a third card, erase the ends of the third blue line and draw three wavy vertical lines on its face. Erase the ends of the fourth blue line from the fourth card and put a square on its face; the fifth blue line from the fifth card, and a five-pointed star on its face.

Now try this: turn all the cards facedown, spread them on the table and mix them around any which way, then look at the back of one of them. Count to yourself from the red line (no matter whether it is now at the left, right, top, or bottom) to the first blue line that has no ends. If it is the first line from the red one, the face of that card has a circle on it; if it is the fourth line from the red one, it has a square on its face.

Try it from a distance. Prop up one of the cards against the back of a chair, as though someone might be holding the card, then stand several feet away from it. You still should be able to see the erased line clearly, so as to tell which one it is from the back.

The reason for erasing both ends of the blue lines is that one end may be partly covered by a spectator's fingers when he holds a card against his forehead, or ends may be overlapped when cards are spread on the table. Don't worry about the fact that the markings seem obvious to you once you know where to look for them. The spectator is kept busy doing things and looking at the faces of the cards. He won't be holding the cards long enough to compare the backs carefully, and even if he should notice that part of a line is missing it will appear to be an imperfection in the printing.

There is no setup for performing. Just have the stack of cards and red marking pen in your pocket or on the table.

What you do:

Explain about the standard ESP symbols and show each of the cards. Hand them all to the spectator, move away, and turn your back, and have him mix them and spread them facedown on the table "so it will be impossible to see what is on

them." Ask him to take any one, look at it, and hold it with
its face against his forehead while he thinks of that symbol.

Face him and look for the red line on the back of the card
he is holding. Mentally count from that to the first blue line
with missing ends. Announce what the symbol is, but don't
make it seem too easy, and have him hold it up to show it to
everybody. Ask him to return that symbol to the table with
the others and to mix and spread them around facedown
again. Turn your back and invite him to take any three
symbols he wishes, to look at them, hold them against his
chest, "and then turn your own back to me."

Turn to face the audience while his back is to you. Pretend
to be having trouble sensing his thoughts. Close your eyes
and put the palm of your hand to your forehead a moment.
Partly cover your eyes to prevent the audience from seeing
the direction of your downward glance as you look down at
the table. Look at the backs of the two cards that remain
on the table. If you see from their backs that those are, for
instance, cards 1 and 3, you know that the spectator is holding 2, 4, and 5 — cross, square, and star. Call each of them and
have him hold them up to show them.

Now turn your back once more while he spreads the facedown cards around on the table to mix them. Then go to the
table, remove the pen from your pocket, and read the back of
each of the cards in turn as you draw red designs on them.
You have plenty of time to figure out each marking. Don't
rush it. Hesitate as you start to make a design on one. Scratch
it out and start over. Say: "I can't get them clearly. . . .
I'm afraid I missed on this — but maybe I got a few."

Finally pick up one of them. Show the audience the face

and then turn it to show your matching symbol on the back. Continue with the others. When you come to the last two, lift them together, one in each hand, with their faces toward you. Glance from one to the other to build suspense, then quickly turn them and hold them up high to show them.

Two Out of Three Isn't Bad

How it looks:

"Some people believe that everybody has extrasensory perception—that we use ESP frequently without being aware of the fact," you say. "Have you ever felt almost certain that you could guess what some person was about to say before he said it? That's a common experience. But is it always only a guess, or is it ESP?"

Taking out some blank cards and a pen, you ask a spectator if he would like to test his possible powers of extrasensory perception in a little guessing game. "It's a game of three guesses. I'll think of three different things and ask you to guess each of them. I don't expect you to get all three. If you could do that, you'd be a mind reader. But perhaps you'll be able to guess one of my three thoughts—or come close to it. Shall we try?"

Holding the cards so he can't see their faces, you write on the top one. "I'm writing the name of a friend of mine, some-one I'm sure you don't know," you explain, "the person's first name. . . ." You put that card facedown on the table without revealing what you have written. "It's a rather com-mon first name. Of course, the person might be a man or a woman. Will you just make a guess? What name came into your mind?"

He may say: "John." You repeat it aloud, write it on the second card you are holding, show it to him, and put that on the table on top of the first card you wrote. "That's your first guess," you say. "Next, I'm going to think of a big city. It might be an American city or a foreign one." You write on the next card and without showing the writing put that on the table. "What city do you guess I have in mind? I'll tell you this much—it's among the one hundred largest cities in the world. Which city do you guess?"

He may guess: "Chicago." You write whatever he says on a card, show it, and put it with the others. "All right. Now the third guess. I'm thinking of a television show—not the name of a particular show, but a much broader category. The kind of a show it is, the type of program, such as comedy or sports, but not those. It's a certain kind of show millions of people watch every night." You write what you are thinking and add that card to the others on the table. "What's your guess?"

He may answer: "The weather report."

You write what he says on the last card you have, pick up the rest of them from the table, and say, "Let's see how well you've done. The television show was the broadest category, so we'll check that one first." You show his card. "You guessed the weather program. . . . No. I'm afraid you missed that one. What I had in mind was the news." You show your card with NEWS on it. "You were very close. I suppose the weather report could be considered part of the news—but to be fair, I think we should call that one wrong."

Putting those two cards aside, you take the next two. "I

thought of a friend's name. Your guess was 'John.' And the name I had in mind *was*—" you show it "—John." Then you take the next two. "You guessed that out of all the cities in the world I was thinking about Chicago. And the city I had in mind *was*—Chicago." The thoughts written on the cards again match. "Two out of three," you say. "That's rather remarkable. Congratulations. Were you only guessing—or did you use your ESP?"

(There is a chance that the spectator may correctly get all three. But at the least, two of his "guesses" will be right.)

What you need:

Six blank cards. These may be any size from business cards to large pieces of poster board, since the routine can be shown close up or to a large audience.

A pencil, pen, or colored marking pen, depending on the visibility required.

The secret and setup:

This is a very simple way of using what is known as the "one-ahead" principle, upon which countless mental-magic effects have been built. Usually the mentalist first asks the spectator to think of something and then appears to read his mind. This presentation is in reverse, in that the performer first writes something and then invites the spectator to "guess" what he has written.

That is done partly to dress up the effect and partly to put the "blame" on the spectator for missing one of three tries. After all, the audience doesn't expect a spectator to be as good at reading minds as the mentalist might be, and the very fact that he may miss one out of three adds to the credibility. It also avoids the use of a direct force, such as with playing cards, dice, or some other device, which is necessary in many "one-ahead" routines.

Sort of a verbal force, which may or may not work, is used. When it does work, the spectator is right all three times. But it isn't essential. The basic principle remains the same. What you write on the first card really matches your third question, and you keep one step ahead of the spectator all the way along, writing his answer each time on the next card instead of what you say you are writing. This will become clear from the presentation.

There are no tricky moves at the end and nothing to prepare in advance. All you need are the six cards and the pen or pencil. You can have them in your pocket or on the table.

What you do:

After introducing the ESP "guessing game," hold the stack of blank cards in your left hand, close to you, and with their faces toward you. Explain that you are writing a friend's name but instead, on the first card, write: NEWS. Be careful not to reveal the writing, and put that card facedown on the table. Say: "It's a rather common first name." This is to keep the spectator from thinking of long or exotic names. "Of course, the person might be a man or a woman. Will you just make a guess? What name came into your mind?"

Repeat aloud whatever name he says, write it on the next card in your hand, show it to him, and put that card facedown on the table on top of the first card. Now tell him you are thinking of a big city. Hold the cards close and write, not the name of a city, but the name of the person that you just wrote on the previous card. Put that card facedown on top of those on the table, continue to talk about the city, and ask him to make his second guess.

Write whatever city he says on the next card in your hand, show it to him as you call it aloud, and put that card facedown on top of the ones on the table. Then tell him you are thinking of a television show, not a particular program, but the kind of a show that it is. Hold the cards close and write, not a TV show, but the city he named. Put that facedown on top of the cards on the table.

Go on talking about the category of TV shows you have in mind, "such as comedy or sports, but not those." By ruling out sports and comedy shows, you have eliminated a lot of possibilities. You now strongly suggest a "nightly" show, a kind almost all viewers regularly watch. "It's a certain kind of show millions of people watch every night," you say. "What's your guess?"

If the verbal force works, he will say, "News." But he may say "Weather" or "Talk show" or something else. Whatever he says, write it on the last card in your hand. Show it to him, then turn its face toward you again, and *keep that card in your left hand.* With your right hand, take all the other cards from the table together, lift them with their faces toward you, and just slide the batch of them *behind* the card you are still holding with your left hand.

There is no "move" to be made. You just casually pick up the cards with one hand and put them into the other as you naturally would. The result is that they are now all stacked in pairs: the two TV guesses, the two names, the two cities. But they are not in the order in which you called for the guesses. So you make an excuse to dispose of the pair facing you first, which are also the ones least likely to be correct.

"Let's see how well you've done," you say. "The television show was the broadest category so we'll check that one first." Turn the stack to show the first card, his TV guess. Whatever he guessed frequently can be called "close," but if he guessed anything but a news program, say that he is wrong. "I'm afraid you missed that one. . . ." Show the next card. "What I had in mind was a news program. I think we'll have to call that one wrong."

Of course if he did guess "News" correctly, you build up to the fact that he got all three right. In any case, you take the next two cards and show that he guessed the person's name, then the last two and show that he guessed the city, and say: "That's rather remarkable. Congratulations. Were you only guessing—or did you use your ESP?"

What's Your Bag?

How it looks:

"I've been exploring the practical uses of psychic phenomena," you say. "There are so many everyday ways that mentalism could be applied if the techniques were developed beyond the area of scientific experiment. For instance—why not put extrasensory perception to work at airline terminals, where baggage is always getting mixed up or lost?"

From a small envelope, you remove four baggage tags, which you lay out on the table around the envelope. On the envelope, you draw a picture of a suitcase. "Let's imagine this is a missing suitcase. It could belong to any of you. The problem is to identify the owner quickly. So why not put a mentalist to work at the baggage counter?"

On each of the tags, you write the name and address of one of the spectators, and invite someone to turn the tags face-down so the names are hidden. "Mix them all up so I have no idea which is which," you say, as you step away from the table and turn your back. "Then spread them all out again."

You return to the table, hold a hand above the facedown tags to "sense the vibrations," and correctly identify each tag, which you pick up and hand to the person whose name is on it. "Applied clairvoyance might accomplish it that way," you explain. "But there are other psychic methods that could be used. Paranormal vision, for example."

Someone now is invited to gather up the tags, mix them thoroughly, and hand the batch of them to you behind your back. "I have no eyes in the back of my head," you say, "but mentally I might try to envision each of your names and match a missing suitcase to its owner." You stand before each person in turn, close your eyes to concentrate, and then bring out the proper tag from those you are holding behind you. "This is yours, Mary. . . . I think your name's on this one, Joe. . . ."

Then you say that it also might be done by "direct telepathy," and explain, "That would be the hardest way to sort out the baggage—if the clerk had no contact at all and simply had to read minds from a distance. But let's try."

You walk to a far side of the room and turn your back. Someone is asked to freely select one tag, without showing the name on it to anyone else, and to put all the other tags into his pocket. Holding that tag before him, he thinks of the name written on it. Standing well away, and with your back to the group, you dramatically reveal the name.

What you need:

Four oblong tags, about 2½-by-4 inches, the kind commonly sold as "household tags." These have a reinforcement tab around the hole at the top where the string is attached.

A small envelope to hold them.

Pen or pencil.

The secret and setup:

This is a combination of three tricks, each accomplished by a different method, all of which depend on the way in which the tags are laid out around the envelope on the table at the start.

The tags are secretly pencil-marked in clockwise order, so you can identify them from their backs by sight. Their tabs are prepared in the same order, so you can tell the tags apart by feeling them when they are held behind your back. They are positioned in such a way on the table that when a spectator later holds up one of them to read what is written on it, he will turn the top of the tag to point in the direction in which it was originally placed on the table. By stealing a quick glance at the tag, from across the room, you can immediately tell which one he holds.

First remove the strings and put the tags on a table in a horizontal row, with their holes at the top. Think of the tags, from left to right, by number: 1, 2, 3, 4. On tag 1, make a small pencil mark at the very top edge of the hole. Pencil mark the right edge of the hole of tag 2, the bottom edge of the hole of tag 3, the left edge of the hole of tag 4. Mark the holes on both faces of each tag.

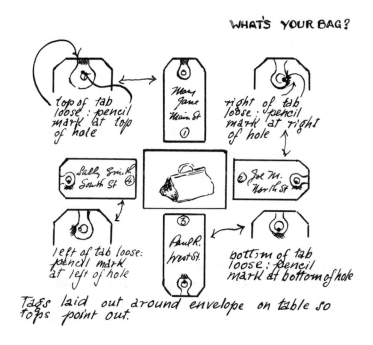

WHAT'S YOUR BAG?

top of tab loose: pencil mark at top of hole

Mary Jane Main St ①

right of tab loose: pencil mark at right of hole

Sally Smith South St ④

Joe M. North St

left of tab loose: pencil mark at left of hole

Paul R. West St ③

bottom of tab loose: pencil mark at bottom of hole

Tags laid out around envelope on table so tops point out.

Next take tag 1 and work your fingernail beneath the top edge of the reinforcement tab around the hole, so as to pull it away from the tag a little and roughen that edge to the touch. Loosen the right edge of the tab of tag 2, the bottom edge of tag 3, the left edge of tag 4. Do that with the tabs on both faces of each tag.

When they are mixed, you now should be able to tell which

is which by sight from the pencil marks. If you hold them be-hind your back, you should be able to identify them by feel-ing around the edges of the tabs with your fingernail. Be sure the markings are clear enough and the tabs are fixed so you can sort the tags quickly by sight or by touch.

Stack the four tags in order — 1, 2, 3, 4 — from the top down, slide them into the envelope, and have that in your pocket with the pen or pencil.

What you do:

Take out the envelope and put it at the center of the table. Remove the tags and lay them out around the envelope like the hands of a clock, with the top end of each tag pointing outward. Tag 1 goes directly above the envelope, with its hole at the top. Tag 2 is placed at the right of the envelope, with its hole to the right; tag 3 at the bottom of the envelope, with its hole to the bottom; tag 4 at the left of the envelope, with its hole at the left.

(This automatically positions the tags so that what is written on each of them will be written in a different direction in relation to the top of that particular tag. Later, when a spectator picks one up, he will have to turn it so that the hole is at the top, right, bottom, or left to properly read what is on it. From the way he holds it, you will know at a glance which tag it is:1, 2, 3, or 4.)

Draw a quick sketch of a suitcase on the face of the envelope, a simple oblong shape with a curved line over it to indicate a handle. Ask four spectators their names and addresses. With-out changing the clockwise position of the tags, write each name on a tag in turn, starting with the one at the top. Include the complete name and address, so the writing covers a considerable portion of the tag, and make the writing small but legible.

As you write the names, remember each person by the number of his tag. For example, if their names are Mary, Joe, Paul, and Sally, think of them as "Mary One," "Joe Two," and so on. There is no need to memorize more than the person's first name.

Step away from the table, turn your back, and invite someone to turn all the tags facedown so none of the names can be seen and to mix them thoroughly. When that has been done, return to the table and hold a hand over the tags without touching them. Pretend to "sense the vibrations" of the hidden names as you secretly look for the pencil dot that identifies each tag so you can hand it to the person whose name is on it.

For the next test, have the tags mixed once more and given to you behind your back. Feel for the tab on the top tag of the batch. Run your fingernail around the edges of the tab to feel where it is loose and secretly learn which one it is. Call the name, give the person the tag, and continue until all the names have been revealed.

Finally suggest "direct telepathy" as the most difficult test of all. Go to a corner of the room, stand with your back to the group, and ask someone to choose any tag without showing the name to the others and to put the rest of them in his pocket. Tell him to hold it up so the writing faces him and to concentrate on that name. Give him time to follow your instructions and then glance around and ask, "Have you done that?"

Immediately turn your head away again. All it takes is a brief glance to spot whether the top of the tag he holds points up, to the right, bottom, or left. You know its number from the position in which it is held, the same position that it was in when you laid the tags out on the table at the start, because the spectator has to turn it that way to read the name written on it. Again, you mentally count clockwise, and reveal the name.

The Head and Tail of It

How it looks:

"Some experiments in extrasensory perception have dealt with how accurately a person may be able to predict the number of times a coin will fall heads or tails," you say, as you invite a spectator to join you in such a test. You hand him a drinking glass, ask him to drop a quarter or any coin from his pocket into it, and then show him what you want him to do. Holding your hand over the mouth of the glass, you shake the coin in all directions, then turn the glass upright and call whether it has fallen heads or tails.

"Try it a few times," you say. "Then we'll run a test series of ten consecutive tosses. Meanwhile I'll attempt to make a prediction."

You write your prediction on a small scratch pad, tear off the slip of paper, fold it, and put it in plain view by sticking the end of the slip into the top of a book that you stand upright on your table. When the spectator says he is ready to start the test, you say, "I'll keep score as you call each toss aloud . . . and everybody — please count to yourselves and keep score of the heads and tails with us."

As the spectator shakes the coin in the glass and calls each toss, you write the results on the pad. When he completes the series of ten, you hand him the pad and say, "Please check this. Just add them up in your mind and see if my totals are correct." Then you ask, "How many times did the coin fall heads and how many times tails?"

He says, perhaps, "Seven and three." You give him your prediction to open and read aloud. He reads: "Seven and three."

What you need:

A tall drinking glass.

A 3-by-5-inch white scratch pad.

A pencil short enough to fit easily into your jacket pocket.

A paperback book.

Three paper clips.

A piece of thick cardboard, such as from a packing carton, cut to a size 4 inches long by 1½ inches wide.

(You should also have a quarter in one of your pockets in case the spectator has no coin of his own to use.)

The secret and setup:

Because of the way they are worded, six prediction slips cover all possibilities. Each slip can be interpreted two ways. A slip that says, SIX AND FOUR, for example, could mean a total of six heads and four tails or six tails and four heads. You lead the spectator, by what you say at the end, to call the totals in the order that you want them called.

The "six-four" slip is the one you write as your prediction during the performance. The other five, to cover the rest of the possibilities, are in a simple index device in your jacket pocket. When you put the pencil into that pocket, you secretly get the needed slip into your fingers and then switch it for the original prediction in a way that will be explained. (Of course, if the spectator should happen to throw a six-four total then no switch is needed, but the slips usually must be switched.)

Start by making up the slips of paper. Put the pad lengthwise on a table. On the first sheet, in capital letters, print: TEN AND NONE. Then, on following sheets: NINE AND ONE, EIGHT AND TWO, SEVEN AND THREE, FIVE AND FIVE. You skip SIX AND FOUR because that will be your original prediction. Tear off each sheet and fold it in half from left to right, in half again, and then from top to bottom.

To understand how the book is used to switch the slips, stand the book upright on end, with the spine to the left. Pick up the pad and write on it: SIX AND FOUR. Tear off the sheet and fold it as you did the others. Stick one end of the folded slip into the top of the book, between the pages, and slide it to the left until it is wedged there with most of it sticking up in full view. That is the way the original prediction will be displayed during the performance.

For now, just to try it, put any of the other folded slips into the right-hand pocket of your jacket. Curl your fingers loosely around it, bring out your hand with the slip concealed by your fingers, and drop your hand naturally to your side. With your left hand, pick up the book and bring it in front of you.

Bring your right hand, with the concealed slip in it, over the top of the book, and with your thumb push the original slip to the right and down between the pages, where it becomes

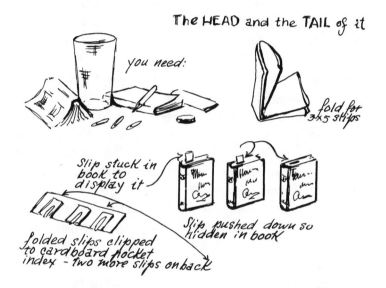

The HEAD and the TAIL of it

you need:

fold for 3×5 slips

Slip stuck in book to display it

Slip pushed down so hidden in book

folded slips clipped to cardboard pocket index - two more slips on back

hidden. Immediately lift that hand to the right and hold it high to show the previously concealed slip, which should be held between your thumb and first finger as if you had merely plucked it from the top of the book. With your left hand, turn the top of the book towards you and drop the book back on the table.

The pocket index to hold the five slips is made with the three paper clips and the piece of thick cardboard. Hold the cardboard lengthwise and fasten the clips to it by pushing them up from the bottom as far as they will go, spacing them left, center and right. Then slide the folded slips into the clips and against the cardboard in order: 10, 9, 8 on one side and 7 and 5 on the other. Push them all the way down into the clips so they remain well-fastened. This index is placed lengthwise in the right-hand pocket of your jacket, with the bottoms of the clips at the bottom and the "10, 9, 8" side toward your body.

Position the index correctly in your pocket and try this: Take the pencil in your right hand, as you will when performing. Put your hand inside the pocket and drop the pencil. Bring your thumb down behind the cardboard, towards your body, and your fingers against the outer side of it. Feel for the slip you want and pull it out of the clip against your fingers. Curl them around it loosely, bring your hand out of your pocket, and drop your hand to your side with the slip concealed in your fingers. This gives you the proper slip to switch for the one in the book.

To set things up for performance, have the loaded index in your right-hand pocket and the pad and pencil in your left-hand pocket. The glass and book are on your table. The book should appear to be one that is just lying there for use in some other routine, not deliberately put there for this.

What you do:

Give the spectator the glass, have him drop the coin into it, and demonstrate what you want him to do. Say, "Try it a few times. Then we'll run a series of ten consecutive tosses. Meanwhile, I'll make a prediction."

Take the pad and pencil from your left-hand pocket. Hold it close so nobody can see what you write and print: SIX AND FOUR. Tear the sheet from the pad, put the pad and pencil on the table, and fold the paper. Glance around as if looking for somewhere to place it. Casually pick up the book, stand it on end, and tuck the folded slip part way into the top and leave it there.

Tell the spectator: "I'll keep score as you call each toss aloud. . . ." Make a score sheet on the pad by printing HEADS at the top left, TAILS at the top right, and drawing a vertical line down the page between them. As he calls each toss, make a mark under the proper heading. When he calls the last one, mark that, and then add them up and write the total at the bottom of each side. Give him the pad and say: "Please check this. Just add them up in your mind and see if my totals are correct."

With your right hand, drop the pencil into your pocket. Think of the higher number of the two totals and get the proper slip from the index into your fingers. Curl your fingers around it, bring your hand out with the slip concealed, and drop your hand to your side. While the spectator is mentally adding the marks on the score sheet to check your totals, pick up the book, make the switch, and hold up the slip that was concealed in your fingers.

The questions you ask him now must be phrased so his answers will match the wording on the slip you are holding. All you have to remember is which total was higher, heads or tails, and ask for that one first.

If he tossed more heads than tails, you ask: "How many times did the coin fall heads?" Wait for his answer. Then ask:

"And how many times did it fall tails?" But if he tossed more tails than heads, you reverse the questions and first ask: "How many times did the coin fall tails?" Then you ask: "And how many times did it fall heads?"

You repeat each of his answers as he gives them, for example: "Seven heads . . . three tails," and then say, "The totals then are seven and three—is that correct?" Hand him the slip. "Will you please read this aloud?—exactly what I predicted?"

He reads: "Seven and three."

Puzzle Me This

How it looks:

"I don't know how many of you are crossword-puzzle addicts," you say, "but for those of you who enjoy doing them the hard way I'd like to suggest this—instead of working out the puzzle with a pencil, try using ESP. . . . I've tried it, but I'll admit that I cheat a little. I need somebody to look at the words and to mentally spell them out for me."

You ask a spectator if he will try it with you and give him a large card on which there is a printed crossword puzzle with its definitions. "It won't be a puzzle for you because all the words are written in," you explain. "You'll see that there are seventy-one definitions and matching words, across and down." From your table, you pick up some cards and spread them in your hands to show them. "On these office file cards, I have printed the letters of the alphabet—two complete alphabets plus a few additional cards for the most commonly used letters."

Turning to the audience, you ask someone to call out any number between one and seventy-one, and then ask the first spectator to look for the word at that number in the puzzle he is holding. "Read the definition to yourself, please," you say, "and then find the proper word, across or down, and concentrate on it. Make sure you have the right one, because I can only get whatever letters are in your mind—and if you are wrong, I will be."

Sorting through the alphabet cards, you remove one, hesitate, and put it back. "I'm not getting your thoughts clearly. . . . So that I will know how many letters I need, will you count the letters in the word to yourself, the number of spaces?—but don't tell me. Let me try to tell you what you're thinking." You close your eyes a moment. "You are thinking seven spaces—a seven-letter word. Am I correct? . . . Good. Now think of just the first letter. I'm getting it now. Think of the next letter, please."

One by one, you draw out letters from the pack of alphabet cards, putting those you choose facedown on the table, and finally putting the rest aside. "I may have missed a letter or two," you say, "but I think I got most of them. . . . First, will you please read the definition of the word aloud—then, very slowly, spell the word for us, letter by letter."

As he spells aloud, you show each of the cards you selected and they match exactly so that you spell out with him the word he had in mind.

What you need:

A fairly large crossword puzzle and its definitions, cut from a newspaper, magazine, or puzzle book. You will also need the printed solution to the puzzle.

Poster board to mount the puzzle upon.

A self-sealing sheet of clear plastic.

A package of 100 blank 3-by-5-inch office index file cards.

A black felt-tip pen.

A rubber band.

Scissors.

The use of a typewriter.

The secret and setup:

All the words of the puzzle are listed by their proper numbers on several typed "cue cards" that are put with the pack of alphabet cards you hold. While searching through the cards for the letters to remove and put on the table, you secretly read the word that matches the number called aloud, and then just draw out the cards to spell that word.

Begin by filling out the crossword puzzle. Work from the definitions and the printed solution. Be careful not to mark over any of the numbers. Write the proper letters with the pen in all the spaces across and down to complete the puzzle. Place the completed and neatly trimmed puzzle, with its accompanying definitions, on a slightly larger piece of poster board. Cut a piece of the self-sealing clear plastic sheet to cover it and smooth that over the puzzle to seal it to the board. This protects it so that the puzzle can be used for many performances.

Make up the pack of alphabet cards, by turning the stack of file cards with their narrow ends top and bottom, and vertically printing one letter of the alphabet on each card. The letters should be large and bold for easy visibility, but there is no need to spend a lot of time drawing them since they are meant to look as though you just quickly penned them. At the top left corner of each card, print the same letter again, much smaller, like the corner index of a playing card, so you won't have to spread out their full faces to find letters you want.

Altogether you will need two complete alphabets of twenty-six letters each, plus two additional *E* cards and one additional card for each of these letters: *A, B, I, O, S.* With those, you can spell almost all words, including the unusual ones often found in crossword puzzles. But add one blank card to the back of the pack. In the unlikely event that you do need some additional letter when performing, just explain to the audience that you have run out of *E*'s, or whatever it is, and take out your pen and make one by printing that letter on the extra blank card.

Use the typewriter to prepare the "cue cards." All the typing should be in capital letters and each line should start at the far left, at the very edge of the card. Take a blank card, roll it into the typewriter with a narrow end at the top, and at the far left type: ACROSS-1. Now look at your completed puzzle, find the first word under the "Across" definitions, space the card down a line, and type the proper number and word, such as: 1-LAMA. Directly beneath that, type the next number and word. Continue until you come to the bottom of the card, then start a second card, and at the top far left of that type: ACROSS-2.

When you have finished all the "Across" words, type cards in a similar way for the "Down" words. All the words in the average puzzle can be typed vertically on four 3-by-5-inch cards, one word to a line. But don't crowd the listings. Use more cards if you need them.

Add the typed cards to the back of all the alphabet cards,

behind the extra blank one. Put a rubber band around the pack of them and have the cards and puzzle on your table.

What you do:

Give the spectator the puzzle. Explain that all the words are written in and that there are seventy-one (or whatever number there are) definitions and matching words, across and down. Pick up the alphabet cards and show some of their faces to the audience as you explain what they are, but don't expose the typed "cue cards" at the back. Square them up and put them on the table for a moment.

Ask someone in the audience to call out any number between one and the highest number in your puzzle. Tell the spectator who is holding the puzzle to look for that number. Repeat the number and say to him: "Look for that number under the definitions for the words that go across. Is there a word that goes across for that number?"

Wait for him to answer. If he says that there *is* an "Across" word for that number, tell him to read the definition to himself, and then to find the proper word in the puzzle and to concentrate on it. But if he says there *is not* an "Across" word at that number, you say: "Then please look for that number under the definitions for the words that go down — read the definition to yourself and then find that word in the puzzle and concentrate on it."

This is important, because for some numbers there are two words, one that goes across and the other that goes down. By asking him to look first at the "Across" definitions, you eliminate the duplicated "Down" numbers. In either case, you learn from his answer whether he is looking at a word that goes across or down. "Make sure you have the right one," you say, "because I can only get whatever letters are in your mind—and if you are wrong, I will be."

Take up the pack of alphabet cards again and hold them close with their faces toward you. As you pretend to look for the letters of the word the spectator has in mind, spread out some of the cards at the right, then some at the center, then spread the typed cards at the back as far as is necessary to read the "cue" words. Because all the typing is at the extreme left edges, you won't have to spread them much.

Look at the "Across" or "Down" listings, as the case may be, for the number that was called from the audience. You have a legitimate excuse to take your time and look directly at the typed cards, since you are supposed to be searching through the alphabet cards for the letters of the thought-of word. When you find the number and matching word, don't try to memorize the entire spelling at once. Remember the first letter of it and count the total number of letters in it to yourself.

Close up the cards, shake your head, and say: "I'm not getting your thoughts clearly. . . . So that I will know how many letters I need, will you count the letters in the word to yourself?—but don't tell me. Let me try to tell you what you're thinking."

Then announce that it is a seven-letter word, or whatever it may be. Ask him to think of the first letter, tell him his thoughts are coming more clearly, and spread the cards with their faces toward you as before. Remove an alphabet card for the first letter and without showing it put it facedown on the table. Again look directly at your "cue card," memorize the next two letters, and after hesitation and fingering of the alphabet cards, remove those letters and put them on the table, facedown on top of the one already there.

Continue until you have chosen all the letters necessary to spell the word. Square up the rest and put the pack aside. Take the chosen cards from the table, hold them stacked together with their faces toward you, and ask the spectator to read the definition of the word aloud. Then have him spell out the word and stress your request to spell it *very slowly*.

Turn the cards one at a time to show the audience each letter. After you show the first, put it face out behind the others in your hand, and continue to do that with the rest, one by one. Match your cards, letter by letter, to his spelling of the word he has in mind.

3

The Mind Controls

The Dice of No Chance

How it looks:

"Does chance alone always decide the numbers that will come up when dice are rolled?" you ask, as you shake a pair of dice and roll them out on the table. "Is there any power of mind that can control the turn of the dice with predictable results?"

Two spectators are invited to join in an experiment and to stand at the sides of the table. Each is asked to take one of the dice. Taking turns, each rolls his single die, calling out the numbers that come up. You write each number as it is called on the face of an envelope in your hand, and show each number written.

"Now let's add all the numbers that turned up by chance," you say, "if it *was* only by chance." You add the column of figures written on the face of the envelope and ask one of the

41

spectators to check your addition and then to call out the total.

He says: "Forty-one."

"Please open the envelope," you tell him. "Inside it, you will find a card. Will you take that out—and read it aloud?"

He removes the card from the envelope and reads: "If the dice *could* be mentally controlled—it might be possible to predict that the total of all the numbers rolled would be exactly . . . forty-one."

What you need:

A letter-sized envelope, about 4-by-7½ inches.

A card that will fit inside it.

Dice with spots large enough to be read easily.

A slip of paper.

A pen that can be clipped into your pocket.

The secret and setup:

You decide on any two-digit number in advance and use that for your prediction. As each spectator in turn rolls his die, you write the number he calls, but you also mentally add them as you go along. Since the highest number that can be rolled with a single die is six, you stop the experiment as soon as the total comes to within six or more of what you predicted. Then when you add the column of figures on the envelope, you secretly write in whatever number is needed so that the total will add up to what you want it to be.

If your predicted number is forty-one, for example, you stop the rolling of dice whenever the total reaches thirty-five or more. At that point the total may be anything from thirty-five to forty. If it happens to be exactly thirty-five, you know you have to add six; if it happens to be thirty-six, you need to add five; if it happens to be thirty-seven, you would add four, and so on. You simply subtract whatever the total happens to be from your predicted total of forty-one and then write in the difference when you add up the column of figures.

But if you wrote it in at the bottom of the column, the spectators might notice that it wasn't the last number rolled. So at the start, when you first begin to write the figures on the envelope, you leave a space beneath the first number. Then when you openly add up the figures, you do it from the bottom of the column up, and when you come to that space near the top, you quickly write in the figure you need. This is covered, as will be explained, by the way you check off each figure with your pen as you add them aloud.

To set things up, choose a two-digit number, somewhere around forty so the rolling of the dice won't be too prolonged. Print your prediction on the card, using that number and the wording given, and put the card into the envelope. Make a note of the predicted total and also of the number that is six less than that so you will know when to stop the experiment. Write them on the slip of paper so you can look at them just before the performance to refresh your memory. Have the envelope and pen in your inside left-hand pocket and the dice in your outer right-hand pocket.

What you do:

(For explanation, the number forty-one will be used as an example of the predicted total.)

Take the dice from your pocket. Shake them and roll them

out on the table as you question whether there is some psychic power that might control the turn of the dice. Have two spectators stand at the sides of the table while you stand between them in back of it. Remove the envelope and pen from your pocket and hold the envelope face up in your left hand with its narrow edges at the top and bottom.

Ask the spectator at your left to pick up one of the dice and tell him to "shake it, roll it out, and call the number."

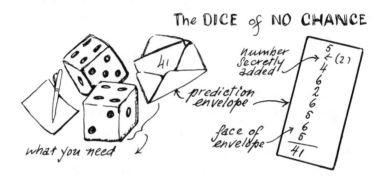

The DICE of NO CHANCE

number secretly added

prediction envelope

face of envelope

what you need

5
← (2)
4
6
2
6
6
6
6
41

Write whatever that number is at the top of the envelope and show him what you have written. Then ask the spectator to your right to take the other die and do the same thing. Write his number on the envelope, but down a little beneath the first one, so there is enough space between them to secretly put in your own number later. Turn the envelope so that the spectator can see what you have written.

Mentally add the first two numbers, and continue to total the numbers in your mind as each spectator rolls his die and you write and show the numbers called. This is easy mental arithmetic since all the numbers are single digits. As soon as your total comes to thirty-five or more, stop the experiment with that roll of the die. Write whatever the last rolled number was, show it to the spectator who rolled it, and say, "Now let's add all the numbers that turned up by chance—if it *was* only chance."

Step back a little so the two spectators can't watch over your shoulders, and hold the envelope close as you bring the pen to it. Add the column of figures from the bottom up and make a small check mark to the right of each figure as you add them aloud. "Three and six are nine . . . and five are fourteen," you might say, making a check to the right of each, "and six are twenty, and five are twenty-five, plus three. . . ."

When you come to the space near the top, write your own number into it, make a check, add it in aloud, and without pausing go on to add aloud the final number at the top of the column. Then draw a line at the bottom and write the total beneath it, but don't say what it is. Turn to either of the spectators, give him the envelope, and say, "Will you check my addition and then call out the total?"

He calls: "Forty-one." You tell him to open the envelope, remove the card he will find inside it, and to please read aloud what it says. He reads your prediction that the rolls of the dice will total exactly forty-one.

Do As I Think

How it looks:

There are three chairs positioned at the front of the room, each with a large numbered card to number them 1, 2, and 3. "I want you, if you will, to walk completely around all three

chairs and then sit in whichever you choose," you tell a spectator brought up from the audience. "Just walk around them
once, make up your mind, remove the number, and sit down."

He sits in, say, chair Number 3. "I have something that I
wish you would keep for a minute or two," you say. "In my
pocket, there is a sealed envelope. Will you remove it, please —
and satisfy yourself that there is nothing else in my pocket?"
Pointing to your pocket, you hold out your jacket so he can
remove the sealed envelope.

From your table, you take another, larger envelope, and
explain that it contains a knife, a fork, and a spoon. "One of
them has something about it that is quite different from
either of the others, as you will see in a moment," you say.
"Because of that, I won't show them to you yet. But I want
you to imagine that you're seated at your dinner table, enjoy-
ing a meal. Which one would you choose to pick up — the
knife, fork, or spoon?"

He may say: "The knife." You take it from the large envelope and give it to him. "I'm glad you chose that one," you
say, "because there's something wrapped around the handle
of it — a little note, from me to you." You remove the fork
and spoon from the envelope and show that there is nothing
wrapped around the handles of either of those. "Will you
open my note, please, and read it aloud?"

The spectator unfastens the rubber band that is snapped
around it, opens your note, and reads: "I am writing this
note twenty-four hours before we will begin our experiment.
I have made up my mind that, when we meet, I shall mentally
direct you to choose the knife you now have, rather than the
fork or the spoon. . . . P.S. — There is something more. . . ."

"Yes, there is something more," you say, as he finishes reading it to the audience. "That sealed envelope you have been keeping since we began this experiment — will you open it up now, please? Take out the card you will find inside it and read aloud what I wrote on it yesterday."

He reads: "I am certain that if you have had your mind open to my directed thoughts — you will now be seated in chair Number 3."

What you need:

Three 7-by-11-inch pieces of white poster board.

A bright red marking crayon.

A knife, fork, and spoon.

Six 3-by-5-inch blank index file cards.

A 9-by-12-inch manila clasp envelope.

Three 2½-by-4¼-inch coin envelopes with end-opening flaps.

Three rubber bands.

A pair of scissors.

The use of a typewriter.

The secret and setup:

There are three sealed predictions, one for each chair, in three different pockets of your jacket, and you simply ask the spectator to remove an envelope from the proper pocket, according to which chair he chooses to sit in. There are also three different predictions for the knife, fork, and spoon — one wrapped around the handle of each. You give him the chosen one with the prediction still wrapped around it, but in removing the other two to show them, you slide their predictions off and leave them hidden inside the big envelope.

Because the routine switches the order of reading the two predictions, the audience should have forgotten by the time the spectator opens the sealed envelope that it wasn't given him to hold until after he sat in the chair that that prediction names. One effect strengthens the other and helps to conceal the very simple methods used in both.

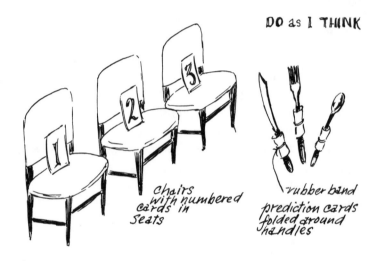

DO as I THINK

Chairs with numbered cards in seats

rubber band
prediction cards folded around handles

Number the poster boards 1, 2, and 3 with the red marker, making each number big and bold. Put one of the blank file cards lengthwise into the typewriter and type the note that will be wrapped around the knife handle, worded as previously explained. Type a second card for the fork, substituting the words ". . . choose the fork you now have, rather than the knife or the spoon," and then type a third card worded to predict the choice of the spoon.

Fold the "knife" card lengthwise from top to bottom, roll

it around the handle of the knife, and fasten it there by winding a rubber band around the outside of the card. Do the same with each of the other cards and the fork and spoon. You will have to experiment a little to discover how tightly the folded cards should be wrapped around the handles so that they won't shake loose and yet can be pushed down off the end easily with your thumb and fingers. The rubber bands provide some "give" for sliding the tubelike cards off the handles. When you have them in place, drop the banded knife, fork, and spoon into the large envelope and fasten the clasp.

Each of the three remaining file cards must be cut to a 2-by-4-inch size with the scissors to fit inside one of the coin envelopes, but it is easier to type the notes on them first and then cut them. Center the typing on them to allow for the cutting. Write the first, with the wording given, to predict that the spectator will be sitting in chair Number 1, the second for chair Number 2, the third for Number 3. Slide one card into each envelope and seal the envelopes.

Put envelope "1" in the outer breast pocket of your jacket, pushed down out of sight, envelope "2" in the inside left-hand pocket, "3" in the inside right-hand pocket. Have the large envelope containing the banded knife, fork, and spoon on your table. Before the performance, position three chairs of any kind so they will be facing the audience, and prop up the number cards in the chairs by resting the bottom end of each card on the seat and the top against the chair back.

What you do:

Explain to the spectator that you want him to walk around the three chairs, make up his mind which he will choose, remove the number card from that one, and sit down. By the time he is seated, you should be standing beside him, holding open the left or right side of your jacket to point to the pocket if the proper envelope is in one of those inside pockets, or else to your outer breast pocket if the envelope you want him to take is there.

Stand at the side of his chair, rather than directly in front of him, so you don't block the view of the audience. Bend down enough so he can reach into your pocket and say, "In my pocket, there is a sealed envelope. Will you remove it, please, and satisfy yourself that there is nothing else in my pocket?" When he has taken it, ask him to keep it "for a minute or two."

Pick up the large envelope from your table and rattle it a little so the knife, fork, and spoon "clink" inside it as you explain what it contains. Turn it so the clasp is toward you and hold the bottom of the envelope with your left hand. Unfasten the clasp with your right hand and spread the top of the envelope wide so you can look down into it but he can't. Tell him one of the three items has something different about it, which is why you won't show it to him yet, and ask him to choose.

When he calls out which one he wants, look down into the envelope, put your hand in, take the chosen one by the end opposite the handle, and bring it out. Hold it up so the audience can see the note banded around the handle as you point it out to the spectator. Ask him to remove the rubber band and unfold your note and read it aloud.

While he is doing that, put your hand into the envelope and take either of the two that remain by the middle of its handle. Inside the envelope, push the banded card down and slide it off the handle with your thumb and fingers, and immediately bring that piece of silverware out. Casually hold it up and show that it has no note wrapped around it, *but don't say anything about it.* Put it into your left hand, which is holding the envelope. Then take out the other one, minus its banded card, to show it in the same way.

When the spectator finishes reading from the note that there is "something more," you say: "Yes, there *is* something more. That sealed envelope that you have been keeping since we began this experiment. . . ." Ask him to open it and read aloud from the card you "wrote yesterday." He reads your prediction that he will be in the specific chair in which he is seated.

Spy Hunt

How it looks:

"Let's imagine we're all secret agents—international spies," you say to four spectators who have been asked to take part in an experiment with you. "We're all hunting for the secret plans that have been hidden among the papers in a hotel room."

You take a paper bag from your pocket, open it up, and spill out on the table five small rolls of paper. "Five little strips of paper, all tightly rolled, each sealed with tape. Please look them over—but don't open any of them yet. You'll see that outwardly they appear identical. But one of these slips— only one—contains the secret plans."

Dropping them back into the bag, one at a time, you mix them thoroughly. "Imagine that the hotel room is dark. It would be too dangerous to turn on the lights. As spies, we are all after the same secret plans — the papers that are somewhere in that room. We all have an equal chance of getting our hands on them — unless one of us somehow might mentally influence the decisions of the others."

You ask each of the spectators in turn to dip his hand into the bag and take out one of the slips of paper. They may change their minds, put back the one taken and choose another, or trade among themselves, until each is satisfied to keep the slip that he holds. "Each of you has chosen one," you say, "and that leaves one for me." You take the last one that remains.

They all unroll their papers and hold them up for the audience to read what is written on them. Printed in large letters on one spectator's strip of paper are the words: LAUNDRY LIST. The others read: SUBWAY MAP, HOTEL BILL, SHOPPING LIST. You unroll yours and show it. On it are the words: SECRET PLANS.

What you need:

Five strips of white paper, each about 15 inches long and 2½ inches wide. You can cut them from a large sheet of paper or use strips from a blank roll of adding-machine tape.

A flat-bottomed brown paper bag, about 5-by-10 inches in size.

Transparent tape.

A broad-tipped black marking pen.

The secret and setup:

Although the strips of paper are rolled and taped so they all look alike to the spectators who casually examine them, the one marked SECRET PLANS is slightly torn so that you can tell it from the others at a glance. When you drop that one into the bag, bend it in half; later secretly draw it up beneath your fingers as you hold the bag at the top. It remains hidden under your fingers while each of the spectators takes one of the other slips from the bag, and at the end it becomes the only one left for you to take.

With the marking pen, in bold black letters as large as will fit on the paper, print the words SECRET PLANS on one of the strips. Roll it up tightly from end to end. Wind a strip of tape around the center to keep it rolled, leaving an end of tape that you can bend down and stick together to form a little tab so it can be pulled loose to quickly open up the roll.

Put that aside a moment and prepare the other strips in a similar way, but print different words on each in turn: LAUNDRY LIST, SUBWAY MAP, HOTEL BILL, SHOPPING LIST. Now take the SECRET PLANS roll, lift one overlapping end, and tear the paper slightly right along the edge of the tape that binds it. A tiny tear is enough—just a fraction of an inch; it should appear accidental, yet you will spot it instantly when that slip is mixed on the table with the others.

Drop that slip and the others into the paper bag, fold the bag, and have it in your pocket.

What you do:

Invite four spectators to join you in the spy hunt for the secret plans and have two of them stand at each side of your table. Open the bag and spill out the rolls of paper as you explain that each strip is sealed with tape and that only one contains the plans.

Rest the bottom of the opened bag on the palm of your left hand. Pick up the papers one at a time with your other hand and put them into the bag. When you come to the one that you recognize as the SECRET PLANS slip, bend it between your thumb and fingers inside the bag as you drop it to the bottom with the others. Just quickly double it, squeezing hard so the two ends touch, and immediately bring your hand out to pick up another slip from the table to drop into the bag.

When you have dropped them all in, shake the bag as you explain that you want to mix them thoroughly. Put your right hand into the bag again and mix the slips around in the bottom, feeling for the bent one. Draw that into your fingers, bring your hand up flatly against the inside of the bag, and take hold of the bag at the top with that hand. Your fingers remain inside at the top, your thumb on the outside, and the slip stays hidden under your fingers, pressed against the inside of the bag at the top.

Holding it that way, shake the bag again, and ask one of the spectators to put his hand in and mix the slips around at the bottom. Have him take out any slip he wishes and tell him, "You can change your mind. Put that back and take another one, if you'd rather." When he is satisfied with the one he has, ask each of the other spectators to reach in and take a slip.

By the time you reach the fourth spectator, there will be only one slip still in the bottom of the bag instead of the two that he thinks are there, because the secret one is hidden

SPY HUNT

slight tear

rolled strip fastened with tape

bent when dropped into bag

Laundry List

Subway Map

Secret Plans

Hotel Bill

Shopping List

fingers hide slip against inside top of paper bag

under your fingers that hold the bag. You are aware of that fact, but he isn't, and to keep him from feeling around in the bag, you hurry him a bit. "Just dip your hand in and take one," you tell him, "and hold it up high."

As soon as he has a slip, move the bag away, shake it, and let the hidden slip drop from under your fingers so it falls to the bottom of the bag. Put the bag on the table and leave it there while you invite the spectators to swap their slips with each other, if they wish. Then say, "Each of you has chosen one—and that leaves one for me."

Let the audience see that your hand is empty by making a casual gesture with it as you speak. Reach into the bag and remove the slip, straightening it between your thumb and fingers inside the bag as you take it out. Don't worry if it remains slightly bent. Just hold it up high and keep it in plain view.

Have each of the spectators unroll his slip. "Open it out between your hands and hold it up so everyone can read it," you say. "What's yours? . . . Oh, I'm sorry—in the dark, you seem to have picked up the laundry list. . . . And you, sir, have a subway map—but not the secret plans we were after. . . . The next gentleman seems to be on his way to do a little shopping. . . . And you're stuck with the hotel bill—I am sorry about that."

Finally you unroll yours and hold it stretched between your hands to display the words: SECRET PLANS.

Mix-Matched Socks

How it looks:

"This is an experiment you might like to try at home—the next time you sort out your laundry," you say, as you display four pairs of socks: black, white, brown, and green. "I can't promise that it will make your household chores easier, but it might make them more interesting. I'm going to ask several of you to attempt to project your thoughts to me—so as to control a series of decisions I will make."

Four spectators are invited to join in the experiment. While your back is to them, each is asked to step up to the table and to select any pair of socks. He is to hide one sock of the pair in his pocket and give the other one to you, behind your back. When all four have done that, you ask the first spectator to take the whole batch of socks you are holding behind your back.

"I want you to keep one of them," you explain, "but not the sock that matches the color of the one you have hidden in your pocket. Some other color—one that doesn't match yours." That spectator then passes the remaining odd socks to the next person, and so on, until each is holding a sock of a different color from the one he has in his pocket. "Now will you all trade with each other—just swap the sock you have for the one your neighbor has? . . . Have you done that? Are you each holding one sock again?"

You then face them, moving along the line as you attempt to determine the color each is projecting in his thoughts, and you sort out the socks, taking a sock from one and handing it to another, changing your mind and shifting the order a few times.

Each spectator finally is left holding one sock. All together, at your signal, they reach into their pockets and bring out the hidden socks to hold beside the ones you have given them. All four pairs match, color for color, down the line.

What you need:

Four pairs of socks: black, white, brown, and green, or any other distinctive colors. They should be of fairly thick material.

A roll of 1-inch-wide double-faced *cloth* adhesive tape (sticky on both sides).

A pair of scissors.

The secret and setup:

The sticky cloth tape is used to make a bead-sized lump inside each sock of a pair in a known position. When each sock is first handed to you behind your back, you know the color of the matching sock that the spectator has hidden in his pocket by secretly feeling for the little lumps. The rest is buildup and presentation.

Since the sticky tape is easily removed, any socks may be borrowed for use as long as they are not transparent when held in the light. For explanation, they will be referred to here by the colors previously listed.

Take the black pair and turn both socks inside out. Cut a 1-inch piece of the double-faced cloth tape and wad it into a tiny ball. Now cut off another 1-inch piece of tape. Put the little ball at the toe of one of the socks, cover it with the second square of tape, and press that firmly to the sock so it stays in place. Then turn the sock right side out and press the tape with your fingers from the outside so it sticks to both inner surfaces. Do the same thing with the matching sock of the black pair.

Fix small lumps of tape in a similar way inside the *heels* of both socks of the white pair, halfway down the *legs* of the brown pair, nearer to the inside *tops* of the green pair. When that has been done, you should be able to learn the color of any sock held in your hands behind your back by running your hand along the length of it from top to toe, remembering that if you feel a lump in the *toe,* it is the black one, and so on for each of the others according to where the lump is.

Roll up each pair, tucked into a neat bundle, and have them all on your table.

What you do:

Display the socks, opening them out to show them, and replace them on the table in pairs. Ask the four spectators to join in the experiment and have them stand two at each side of the table. Explain to the first spectator on your right that you want him to select any pair he wishes without letting you see them. Move forward a few steps, so your back is toward the table and the four spectators but you are facing the audience. When he says he has chosen a pair, tell him: "Please hide one of those socks in your pocket—either one of the pair—and then hand me the other behind my back."

Take the sock from him, keeping your hands behind you, and instruct the second spectator to do the same thing. While he is following your instructions, feel for the lump in the sock the first spectator has given you. Do it casually, by pulling it through your fingers as if you were unconsciously toying with it as you talk. Mentally tag the first spectator according to the sock you know he has chosen. For example, if you feel a lump in the toe you know it is black and that he has the matching black one in his pocket, so you think of him as "Mister Black."

By now, you have taken the sock from the second spectator, and you feel for the lump in that and mentally think of him, say, as "Mister Brown" or "Mister Green." Continue in the same way with the two spectators standing at the left of your table.

Finally give the whole batch of socks to the first spectator, keeping your back toward him as he takes them from you. Tell him you want him to keep one of the socks, but not one the same color as the sock he has hidden in his pocket. "Mix them all up and take any one," you say, "but some other color—one that doesn't match yours. Then please hand the rest of them to your neighbor."

Have each of the remaining spectators do the same. Then tell them to trade socks with each other, swapping them down the line. Give them time to do that and ask, "Are you each holding one now?"

Turn to face the spectators and say: "Perhaps the one you are now holding happens to match the one you have hidden in your pocket. Maybe so—maybe not. But I want each of you to please think of the color of the sock hidden in your pocket—not the color of the sock in your hand, but the one in your pocket. . . . Your thoughts will control the decisions I make."

Move from one to another. If the sock he holds doesn't match the one you know he has in his pocket, take it from him and give it to the person who does have that color in his pocket, switching them around from person to person until you know they all match. Pretend to make a mistake. Change the order a few times.

Step to the side and say: "I believe I have read your thoughts. I'm not sure. Maybe I haven't gotten all of them."

Hold up your hand. "When I snap my fingers, will you all please reach into your pockets and pull out the socks you have been hiding there?" Snap your fingers. "Now. All together— hold both hands up high, please." Look at them a moment and then turn to the audience. "They do match. All of them. Four out of four."

4

From Mind to Mind

Telepathy for One

How it looks:

You are alone with one of your friends, someplace where the person can sit at a table directly across from you, and you turn the conversation to psychic phenomena and telepathy.

"If you came up to me on the street and challenged me to read your mind, I know I couldn't do it," you say, "because you might be thinking any of hundreds of different things and I wouldn't know where to start. But if we both agreed in advance that you were to think of something specific—such as somebody's name. . . . Let's try it. Just for fun."

From your pocket, you take out a wallet, and sort through the cards in it until you find one with a blank side. "This will do," you say, pushing the card across to him, and giving him a pen or pencil if he hasn't one. "I'll turn my head and you just print a name on the card. Print the name of someone

63

you're sure I don't know. Then turn the card so the writing is facedown and put it at the center of the table."

You turn your head or stand up and turn your back to him. When he says he has written the name and turned the card over, you sit facing him across the table again. "I'll cover it with this," you say, picking up the wallet and dropping it on top of the card. "I want you to imagine that there is a big red spot, right here." You point to the face of the wallet. "Fix your eyes on that to center your thoughts and then concentrate on the name."

Slowly you begin to "read" his thoughts. You get one letter of the name, then another, and finally reveal the entire name.

What you need:

A large "secretary-type" wallet, about 4½-by-8 inches in size, with a pocket inside that will hold an assortment of cards.

Half a dozen business cards. Preferably these should be cards of various kinds and sizes, some with one side blank and some penciled with notes, such as normally might be carried in a wallet.

Double-faced (sticky both sides) transparent tape.

A pen or pencil.

The secret and setup:

The wallet has a small strip of double-faced tape stuck to one face of it. When you cover the person's card with the wallet and point to an imaginary red spot, the card sticks to the bottom of the wallet. You tilt the wallet up on edge as you explain how you want the person to center his thoughts on the "spot," and the card lifts with it so you can secretly read the name he has written on the card.

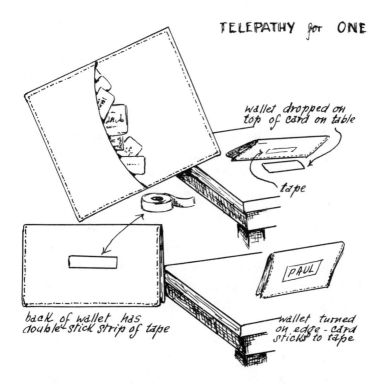

TELEPATHY for ONE

wallet dropped on top of card on table

tape

back of wallet has double-stick strip of tape

PAUL

wallet turned on edge - card sticks to tape

There is little to prepare. Start with the wallet on a table, turned like a book you were about to read, narrow ends top and bottom. Fasten a 1½-inch strip of double-faced tape vertically to the outside center of that face of the wallet. Rub the ball of your thumb over the tape a few times to make it slightly less sticky. Then open the wallet and put the assorted cards inside it.

Put the wallet into the inside right-hand pocket of your jacket, so the taped side of it is toward your body, with the open edges of the wallet at the rear of the pocket. Have the pen or pencil clipped into that pocket.

What you do:

With your friend seated directly across from you at a table, remove the wallet from your pocket with your left hand. Keep it upright, tape at the back. Transfer it to your right hand and put it on the table with its taped side down so that its *long* edges are at the top and bottom. Open it, sort through the cards, select one with a blank side, close the wallet, and leave it in that lengthwise position.

Slide the card, blank side up, across the table to him. Ask if he has a pen or pencil, and if he hasn't, give him yours. Turn your head or stand with your back to him and say, "Just print the name on the card. Print the name of someone I don't know." You are telling him twice to "print" the name, to avoid handwriting that might be difficult to read quickly. "Then turn the card so the writing is facedown and put it at the center of the table."

When he has done that, sit facing him again and say, "I'll cover it with this." Pick up the wallet with your right hand at the long edge that is toward you and drop it on top of the card. As you do, glance to see that the tape will come in contact with the card. The wallet should lie horizontally, covering the card lengthwise.

"I want you to imagine that there is a big red spot right

here," you say. Point to the center of the wallet and press down with the tip of your finger so that the card beneath it sticks to the tape. With your left hand, tilt the wallet up without lifting it off the table, and continue to tap the face of the wallet with your right finger, pointing to the imaginary "spot." Tell him, "Fix your eyes on that to center your thoughts and then concentrate on the name."

As you speak, secretly look at the card that is stuck to the back of the up-tilted wallet and read the name he has printed. You should be able to gain the information at a glance, even if the printing appears upside down to you, which sometimes happens. The instant you know what the name is, immediately drop the wallet flat so that it lies over the card again.

Pretend to get one or two letters and finally reveal the entire name. With your left hand tilt up the wallet, and bring your right hand underneath to flick the card free of the tape with your fingers. Lift the wallet away with your left hand, pick up the card with your right hand, and turn the card over. Read the name aloud as if to confirm that you "read his mind" correctly, and put the wallet away in your pocket as you hand him the card, to keep if he wants it.

Needle in a Mental Haystack

How it looks:

"In this dictionary there are more than seventy-five thousand words," you say, as you show a paperback dictionary and hand it to one of a group of spectators. "In a moment, I will ask you to open it to any page at all . . . and to choose any word at all from that page. When you have decided on a word — don't say it aloud, don't even whisper it. Just point to it on the page and show it to the person seated at your right."

You turn to that person seated next to him. In your hand, you have a self-erasing Magic Slate, the kind with a plastic face on which things that are written can be erased simply by lifting up the top plastic sheets. "What I want you to do is to copy down that word he points to and show it to a few of the others around you, so that you will all have it in your minds," you explain. "Then erase what you have written — like this — so the word remains only in your minds."

To demonstrate, you write something on the Magic Slate and lift the top sheets to erase it, then give him the slate and move away with your head turned. "All right. . . . Open the dictionary. Any page — any word. Have you found one? Point to it on the page so your neighbor is sure which one you mean. . . . And you, sir, will you copy it on the slate, please, and show it to the others near you — then erase it? Have you done that?"

You take back the dictionary and plastic slate and return to the front of the room. "I'm sure you'll agree that for me to search through your minds to find one word out of seventy-five thousand is a little like searching for a needle in a mental haystack — which is why I wanted more than one of you to think of that word. Will you think of it now, please, as I turn these pages, and try to guide me to it mentally."

Opening the dictionary, you turn it to a page, glance at the words, shake your head, and turn to another page.

"Let's try it another way," you say, putting down the diction-ary. "Just think of the first few letters in the word."

You pick up the slate, show it blank, write a letter or two, then erase and start over. You write several more letters, show them, and ask, "Am I right so far?" Taking the dictionary again, you turn the pages, finally run your finger down a page and stop. Aloud, you hesitantly begin to spell out the letters. Quickly, you take up the slate and print the correct word across it. "One word in seventy-five thousand," you say. "Is that the word?"

What you need:

A self-erasing plastic surfaced Magic Slate, about 6-by-8 inches. These are available in stationery stores and at toy counters. You will also need the plastic writing stylus that comes with it.

A paperback pocket dictionary.

Some facial tissues.

The secret and setup:

Although lifting the top plastic sheets instantly erases the visible writing on a Magic Slate, a clear impression of it remains on the black waxed backing directly beneath. By gently rubbing and polishing that waxed black surface with a tissue before the performance, all previous marks can be removed. When the spectator writes the word and erases it, the impression of the word remains, hidden under the top plastic sheets.

Each time you attempt to write a few letters while trying to "read" the spectators' thoughts, you naturally lift up the top sheets to clear the slate, and you secretly glance at the impression of the word on the backing beneath. This can be done several times if necessary when the word is a long one and the spelling difficult to remember.

Try the slate by writing any word with the stylus, then lifting the top sheets to clear it. Hold the plastic sheets up and you will see the impression of the word on the waxed black backing. By tilting the slate very slightly, depending on the light, you can make the writing seem to stand out even more boldly.

When performing, hold the slate with your left hand, upright with its surface facing you. With your right hand lift the top sheets straight up all the way to erase the slate and also to give you a clear view of the backing, and then release the sheets so they fall down into place again.

To clear the slate of the practice word you wrote, crumple a tissue and gently rub it over the black surface, polishing the wax clean. Have the slate, stylus, and dictionary on your table.

What you do:

Take the slate and stylus in your left hand and the dictionary in your right hand and approach the group of spectators. Give the dictionary to one of them and explain that in a moment you will ask him to open it to any page and to select any word. Explain that he is not to say the word aloud, but is just to point to it on the page and show it to the person next to him.

Turn to the second spectator and explain that you will want him to copy the word that is pointed out to him, to show it to those around him, and then to erase what he has written. Demonstrate by printing a short word at the top of the slate and to the side, and then lift the plastic sheets to erase it. Give him the slate and stylus, move away and turn your head.

Ask the first spectator to open the dictionary "to any page — any word" and repeat your instructions that he is to say nothing, but just to point to the word and show it to his neighbor. Tell the second spectator again to copy that word, show it to those around him, and then erase it. When they say they have done that, take back the dictionary, slate, and stylus and return to the front of the room.

Keep the dictionary in your hands, but toss the slate on the table as if it were no longer of any importance, and drop the stylus into your pocket. For the next few moments ignore the slate entirely. Open the dictionary and turn the pages, pretending to try to read the thoughts that will guide you to the word. Admit you are having difficulty. As if the idea just occurred to you, say, "Let's try it another way." Put down the dictionary and pick up the slate. "Just think of the first few letters in the word."

Take the stylus from your pocket. Hold the slate upright and facing you. Lift the top sheets as if to clear it and glance at the impression of the word on the waxed black backing beneath. Try to catch at least a letter or two at first glance, but don't stare at it. Immediately drop the sheets again, turn the slate to the audience to show it blank, and print any letters on it that *do not* suggest the chosen word. Print them up high or down low, not over the area of the slate where you know the hidden impression is.

Show what you have written, questioningly look out at the

spectators, and then say, "No. I'm wrong—that's not how the word starts." Turn the slate to face you, clear it again, and steal a second glance at the word. Then print the first few letters of it. Show the slate and ask, "Am I right so far?"

When you are sure of the word, put the stylus and slate on the table and pick up the dictionary. Look for the word in it. Turn the pages, run your finger down the columns, turn another page or two. Finally stop at the right page.

Point your finger to the word. Start to spell it aloud. Throw down the dictionary, quickly pick up the slate, hold it towards the audience, and boldly print the correct word across the slate for everyone to see as you say: "One word in seventy-five thousand. . . . Is that the word?"

What's in the News?

How it looks:

You pick up a newspaper and give each of three spectators a double-page sheet of it, keeping one yourself to demonstrate what you want done. "Just tear a piece about this size from any part of any page," you explain as you rip a piece from your paper. "Top, bottom, front, back. It doesn't matter what pieces we use. Then crumple the piece into a ball like this."

To show them, you crumple yours into a ball and drop it into a glass, in which you collect the rest of the pieces. One of the spectators is invited to return to your table with you. You pour the balled-up pieces out of the glass, and he chooses one, which he opens and reads to himself while you stand well away from him.

You then "read his mind" to reveal what the news story is about. He concentrates on the headline, and you tell what it is. He is asked to think of the name of any person who happens to be mentioned in the news item, and you reveal that name. Finally, he mentally spells out one of the words to himself, and you spell it aloud with him, letter by letter.

What you need:

A newspaper, preferably tabloid size for easy handling.
An "iced-tea" glass, about 6 inches high.
A large pad and broad-tipped marking pen.
A pencil.

The secret and setup:

Although the presentation leads the audience to imagine that any part of the newspaper might have been chosen, you actually do the "choosing" yourself, and the spectator gets a news item you have read and made notes from in advance.

Start by looking through the paper you intend to use for a news item that meets these conditions: It should be at the top of the outside column of a right-hand page as you open the pages before you; the item should have a solid advertisement or picture on the back of it, not another news story or reading material; it should mention the names of only two or three people.

When you have found the news item you want, read it through a few times and remember as much about it as you can. At the top of the first sheet of the large pad, lightly pencil the headline, then list the personal names mentioned in the item with a one-word reminder for each to indicate who they are or what they do, and finally make a note of the very last word in the item.

Now remove the outside front double page of the paper and three more pages. Put the double sheet that contains your news story inside those, and then put the rest of the paper inside your page at the center. Refold the paper and have it on your table with the glass, the facedown pad and the marking pen.

What you do:

Show the newspaper and discard the front page as you explain: "We won't use the big headlines for this. Let's get down to the fine print." Peel off the next three double pages from the outside of the paper, one at a time, and give one to each spectator. Remove the fourth double page and put aside the rest of the paper.

As you demonstrate what you want the spectators to do, open out the double page you are holding. Unknown to the audience, the piece you want to save is at the top of the right-hand column. Just tear it out as you say: "Tear a piece about this size from any part of any page. Top, bottom, front, back. It doesn't matter what pieces we use." Don't try to be precise or fussy about the tearing. Make it seem casual, as if you were merely ripping any piece from the paper. Hold the piece up for them to see its size and crumple it up into a ball at least as big as a golf ball as you continue to show the spectators what to do.

While they are doing that, pick up the glass and drop your ball of paper into it. Then take the glass to the spectators and have each of them drop in their balled-up pieces. Because you put yours in first, it naturally remains at the bottom, so there is no difficulty in remembering which it is. Invite one of the spectators to return to your table with you. Tip the glass and spill the balls of paper out on the table, watching to see where yours falls.

Ask the spectator to pick up any two of them. If one of the two he picks up is yours, say: "All right. Now hand me one of those — either one you choose." But if neither of them that he first picks up is yours, say: "All right. We've eliminated two. Just throw those away. Now pick up the other two and hand me one of them — either one you choose."

Whichever way he starts, you have now brought him to the point of handing you either the piece you want or of keeping that and handing you the other one. If he hands you the one you want, you say: "Okay. We'll use this one then. You can throw the other one away." But if he gives you the other one, simply throw it away yourself and point to the one he still has in his hand as you say: "That's the one you've chosen to keep."

Tell him to unroll the ball of paper as you turn away from him. "Open it up and read either side of it to yourself," you say. "It doesn't matter which side you choose as long as there's a news item on it — a few paragraphs of information of some kind." Since there was only a picture or solid advertisement on the back of the chosen piece, he is forced to read the side you want him to read. "Is there enough of the story there so that you can get an idea of what the news item is about?"

Close your eyes a moment and then, haltingly and in general terms, begin to reveal the subject of the news item aloud. Talk around it and gradually describe some of the details you remember. Pick up the pad and marking pen and say, "It may help if I try to jot down some of your thoughts as they come to me."

Hold the pad upright facing you and scribble a few words as you continue to talk about it. As you do, glance at your penciled notes at the top of the pad. Ask if the item includes a headline. Have him concentrate on it. Scribble again and then tell him what the headline is, not word for word, but the gist of what it says.

Ask him to glance through the item and to think of some person whose name may be mentioned in it. If there are three names, you will now have to fish a little to find out which one he is thinking about. From the notes on your pad you know the three possible names, so you call out an initial or describe who a person is or what he does—keeping it vague until you know you have hit on the one he has in mind. Then quickly reveal the full name as you scribble it on the pad. While you are doing that, memorize the final note on your pad, the spelling of the last word in the news item.

"Now please look at the last sentence—the very last word," you say. "In your mind, spell that word slowly—to yourself."

Throw the pad facedown on the table. Face him directly and spell the word aloud as if you were receiving his thoughts one letter at a time. Repeat the word and ask: "Am I right? Was that the exact word you had in mind?"

First the Answer—
Then the Problem

How it looks:

You tell the audience that all evening long you have been receiving a strong mental impression of a number. "It keeps popping into my mind. I can see it clearly, but I don't know what it means." You write the number on a slate and show it to them.

"Does it have any special meaning to anybody?" you ask. "Somebody's phone number—part of the license number of somebody's car?" There is no response. "No? ... I guess not." You shake your head and put the slate, number side down, on the table. "Never mind. Let's forget it. We'll go on to something else. ... I'd like to try an experiment dealing with the years of your birth–your birthyears."

Three spectators are asked, in turn, to write the year they were born on the first page of a small memo book that they pass from one to another while your head is turned so that you can't see what is written. The last spectator is asked to close the cover. Holding the closed notebook high in your hand, you return to your table.

"I'm going to attempt to get a mental impression of each of these three years," you say, "and mentally add them together so that the unknown total—" You interrupt yourself. "Wait a minute. This is very strange. There's something happening here that I don't understand. It's like having an answer before I know the problem."

Quickly you go to a fourth spectator, open the notebook, and ask him to add the three birth years, and then to call the total aloud. He does and it is the same number you wrote on the slate at the start.

"That's where that number came from," you say, as you pick up the slate and show it. "The number that kept popping into my mind all evening — before I knew the years when any of you were born. You weren't consciously thinking of those dates when I started to see that number in my mind — but perhaps the years of our lives are always subconsciously in our thoughts."

What you need:

Two identical small (about 3-by-5-inch) memo books, the kind with a spiral wire binding at the top and with stiff, but fairly thin, brightly-colored covers.

Slate and chalk.

Double-faced (sticky both sides) transparent tape.

A pencil and scissors.

The secret and setup:

The memo book is prepared so that you can switch pages. The years the spectators write are on a page that will be hidden by a double-cover device. On another page are three dates you have secretly written in advance. Those are the ones that are finally added up to give the total first shown on the slate.

Start by removing the colored cover from one of the memo books, tearing through the perforations that hold it to the spiral wire at the top. Discard the rest of that memo book. With the scissors, carefully trim away the torn perforations at the top edge of that cover. Then trim a tiny edge from the sides and bottom so that the entire duplicate cover is just slightly smaller than the paper pages of the second memo book.

Open the second book flat. Turn back four of the paper pages. With strips of the double-stick tape fasten the loose

FIRST the ANSWER - then the PROBLEM

duplicate cover to the *rear* of the fourth paper page. When the duplicate cover is in place, it should look like the inside front cover of the memo book. But between it and the real cover there are four paper pages. Those pages should hide the fake cover when the book is opened to the first page.

On the fifth page of the prepared memo book write any three years you choose, one beneath another so they may be added up later. Keep them within a reasonable age range and try to make it look as if the three numbers had been written by different persons, by making the sets of figures seem in different handwriting. On a separate scrap of paper, add the three dates. Lightly pencil the total on the wooden frame of the slate.

Close the memo book and have it on your table with the pencil and the slate and chalk.

What you do:

Secretly glance at the penciled number on the slate frame as you pick up the slate. Talk about the number that keeps "popping into my mind." Write that number in chalk across the face of the slate and ask if it has any special meaning to anyone in the audience. When you get no response, put the slate on the table with the number side down, and pretend to go on with another experiment.

Pick up the memo book and pencil and approach the first spectator. Open the real cover, turn it underneath the pad, and hand him the book and pencil. Ask him to write the year he was born while you turn your head away. Then have him pass the memo book to a spectator next to him. Tell that person to jot his birth year down directly beneath the first one. Have him hand the memo book to a third spectator, who is asked to write the year of his birth "right under the first two." Instruct the third one to close the cover of the book so that you can't see what has been written.

Take it from him, hold your hand high so the memo book remains in full view, and return to your table. Explain that you are going to attempt to get an impression of each of the three years and then add all three together mentally to reach a total. Break off your explanation. Say that "something strange" seems to be happening, as though you were getting an answer before you know the problem. Act puzzled about it and quickly approach a fourth spectator, one who is *seated at a distance from the first three.*

As you do, open the memo book to the *duplicate* cover. It is easy to locate because of its thickness beneath the extra pages on top. Swing that duplicate cover right over the top of the spiral binding and bring it underneath the book, turning the extra top pages and real cover with it, as if merely opening the book again. Don't make a tricky move of it; just open the book there, give it an outward flip, and the real cover and top pages will all flip over together with the fake cover.

The audience has a brief glimpse of the back of the duplicate cover and assumes that you are opening the real cover to the first page. Actually the page you now show the fourth spectator is the one on which your own set of figures was written. Turn the memo book so the figures face him, with the covers held under it. Give him the pencil and have him add the numbers while you hold the book for him. Ask him to write down the total and call it aloud.

Take the memo book with you and go back to your table. Read the total aloud again from the book. Turn the slate and show the number on it as you say, "That's where that number came from. . . . The number that kept popping into my mind all evening—before I knew the years when any of you were born."

A Walk Through the Yellow Pages

How it looks:

"You can find almost anything in the yellow pages of the phone directory—hundreds of all kinds of products and services," you say as you show a phone book and hand it to someone in the audience. Pointing to another spectator, you ask, "Will you please call out any letter of the alphabet from *A* to *Z*?"

He calls out, say, the letter *C*. The person holding the book is asked to open it to the yellow pages that start with that letter. "Just look through them for the first main heading that begins with a *C*—whatever type of business that may be. Turn the pages until you find that first heading with the names and phone numbers of various companies of that kind listed beneath it."

You hold up a large card that has a rough sketch of a telephone dial drawn at the top. "I want you to look at this phone dial and imagine that you are dialing the number of the first company listed under that heading," you explain. "Don't say anything aloud. Dial it mentally. Think of one number at a time—and dial it slowly, please."

Taking a pen from your pocket, you print a phone number on the card in large red numerals and ask, "Is that the number you dialed in your mind?" When he says that it is, you ask him to think of the kind of business or service he is calling, and you print on the card, say, CABINET MAKER. He again confirms that you are correct.

"Now when somebody answers your mental phone call," you say, "what name will you ask for? What company or person are you calling? Will you please think of that name — but don't tell me." After a moment's concentration, you write on the card, say, PAUL GREGORY & SONS. For the third time, the spectator agrees that you have correctly read his thoughts.

What you need:

A classified phone directory or a phone book with a classified yellow page section in the rear.

A large blank white piece of cardboard, about 8-by-14 inches.

Two 3-by-5-inch blank index file cards.

A broad-tipped black marking pen.

A red marking pen that can be clipped into your pocket.

Transparent tape.

The use of a typewriter.

The secret and setup:

The listings are limited to a total of twenty-six by the fact that one letter of the alphabet is called for and the first category, number and name under that letter are used. The information for all twenty-six possible choices is typed on two cards taped to the back of the large one, on which the phone dial is drawn.

When you hold the large card in front of you so the spectator can "mentally dial the number," you read the information to yourself from the back of the card. The routine gives you a logical excuse to hold up the "phone dial" card three times, so you don't have to remember everything at once.

Turn the large card so its narrow edges are at the top and bottom. Near the top draw a rough sketch of a phone dial with the black pen. Start by making an outer circle about 5 inches in diameter. Inside that draw another circle about 3½ inches in diameter. Between the two circles print large numbers from 1 to 0, spaced around from right to left as they are on a phone dial. Beneath each number, inside the smaller circle, draw another little circle of about ½ inch in diameter. These represent the finger holes of the dial. At the center of the whole thing, where the head of the screw that holds the dial would be, mark a black dot.

Roll one of the file cards, with its narrow edges top and bottom, into the typewriter. Open the phone book and find the first *main heading* in the yellow pages that starts with the letter *A* and that has a listing of companies and phone numbers directly beneath it. (Ignore any minor cross-index headings in small print that may refer to listings on other pages.)

At the top of the file card and as far to the left as the typewriter will allow, type the letter *A* and then the kind of business given in the heading, for example: A-ACCOUNTANTS-CERTIFIED PUB. Space down a line and type the first listed name and phone number, such as: ADAMS, GORDON-528-2873.

Then look in the book for the first main heading that starts with *B* and type that information—and so on until all twenty-six listings for each letter of the alphabet are typed on the two file cards.

Turn the large "phone dial" card facedown and attach the two typed file cards, side by side, to the back of it near the top. Attach them with short strips of tape top and bottom so

A WALK THROUGH the YELLOW PAGES

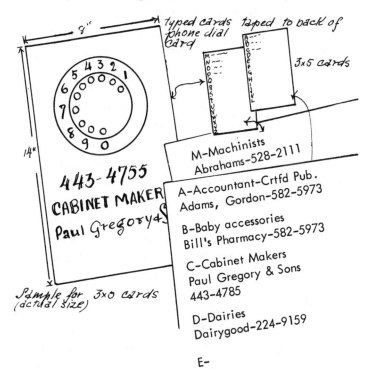

typed cards taped to back of phone dial card

3x5 cards

9"

14"

443-4755
CABINET MAKER
Paul Gregory &

Sample for 3x0 cards
(actual size)

M–Machinists
Abrahams–528-2111

A–Accountant–Crtfd Pub.
Adams, Gordon–582-5973

B–Baby accessories
Bill's Pharmacy–582-5973

C–Cabinet Makers
Paul Gregory & Sons
443-4785

D–Dairies
Dairygood–224-9159

E–

you can remove them later to use with a fresh large card and won't have to retype all the information for each performance.

Have the prepared "phone dial" card faceup on your table and the red pen clipped into the inside left pocket of your jacket.

What you do:

Show the phone book and give it to someone in the audience. Have someone else call out any letter of the alphabet, then ask the person with the book to look in the yellow pages for the *first main heading* for any kind of a business or service that begins with that letter. Make sure he understands that you want him to find a heading with a listing of company names and numbers beneath it. Wait for him to locate it and say again, "The first main heading that begins with a *C*," (or whatever letter may have been called from the audience).

Ask him to look for the phone number of the first company listed under that heading. Pick up the large card and hold it upright in front of you so the dial faces the spectator and the audience. Hold it so you have a clear view from the back of the small cards with the information typed on them.

"Now I want you to look at this phone dial and imagine you are dialing that number," you explain. "Don't say anything aloud. Dial it mentally. Think of one number at a time – and dial it slowly in your mind."

While you are speaking, look at the back of the card and memorize the phone number listed under that letter of the alphabet. Look only for the number, not the rest of the listing yet. Turn your body a little to the left and hold the card, still upright and facing the audience, with your left hand so that the back of the card is cradled against your left arm. With your right hand remove the red pen from your pocket.

Pretend to "receive" the number the spectator is mentally dialing. Print it with the red pen in large numerals across the face of the card and beneath the drawing of the dial. Ask: "Is that the number you dialed?"

When the spectator says that it is, ask him to look at the dial again and to think of the kind of business or service he is calling. Hold the card in front of you so he can "concentrate his thoughts" on the dial. Glance at the back of the card for the proper listing, remember it, and then hold the card as before against your left arm while you print the kind of a business across the face of it, beneath the phone number. Ask him to confirm it.

"Now when somebody answers your mental phone call," you say, "what name will you ask for? What company or person are you calling?" Hold the card in front of you again so the dial faces him. Look on the back for the listing of the name and remember it. "Will you please think of that name?"

Shift the card so its back is against your left arm. Write the name beneath the number and kind of business, then ask once more if you are correct. For the third time, the spectator says that you are.

The Silent Commercial

How it looks:

Showing a folded slip of paper, you ask a spectator who is standing beside you, "May I put this in your pocket?" Tucking it into the top of his breast pocket, you say: "We are about to conduct a marketing survey. . . . But first—we'll have to take time out for a commercial."

You stand silent for a moment with your eyes closed, and

then open them and say: "There—the commercial's finished. You didn't hear it because it was a silent commercial. There were no pictures to watch because it was an invisible commercial. It was in my mind—and perhaps it is now in your mind, too, even though you may not be aware that you heard any commercial message at all."

From your pocket, you take four metal-rimmed cardboard discs and explain that on each of them you have written the name of a breakfast cereal. You ask the spectator to take them and read them aloud, and he reads: "Flakes, Crackles, Toasties, Crunchers."

"My sponsor is the manufacturer of one of those four brands," you say, "and our survey is to test whether silent commercials work—whether you have been mentally influenced to buy that brand instead of one of the others—so that you will reach for my brand by some blind impulse."

You drop all the discs into the side pocket of your jacket and hold it open wide as you invite the spectator to dip his hand in and take one of them. "Mix them up. Don't take the first one you touch—unless you want to. . . . You have one? Will you please read the name on it aloud?"

He reads: "Toasties." You then ask him to remove the slip of paper that you put in his breast pocket at the start and to read that aloud. He reads: "Thank you for listening to my silent commercial. My sponsor will be pleased that you bought—Toasties."

What you need:

Eight round metal-rimmed blank cardboard tags, 1¾ inch in diameter, with their strings removed.

A sheet of paper from a small scratch pad.

A black felt-tip marking pen.

A jacket with a small "ticket pocket" just inside the top of the right-hand pocket. Most men's jackets are made with such a pocket.

The secret and setup:

There are four duplicate tags, all with the same name on them, in the bottom of your right-hand jacket pocket. The other four, with various names on them, are shown to the spectator and then are dropped into the little "ticket pocket" inside the top of your right-hand pocket. You hold your hand over that as you spread the rest of the pocket wide so that he may dip his hand into it. He is forced to "choose" one of the four duplicates from the bottom of the pocket, which bears the name that was written on the slip of paper given to him at the start.

Print the four breakfast cereal names, or any other product names you may wish to use, on four of the tags. Then print one of those four names, TOASTIES for example, on all four of the other tags. Write the prediction note, worded as explained, on the sheet of paper from the scratch pad and fold it in half.

Drop the four duplicate tags, all with the same name on them (TOASTIES), into the bottom of your right-hand pocket. Put the other four, all with different names on them, into the little "ticket pocket" along with the folded slip of paper.

What you do:

Have the spectator stand to your right. Remove the prediction slip from your pocket. Show it without opening it and ask if you may put it in his pocket. Tuck it into the top of his breast pocket so part of it remains in view.

Say that you are about to conduct a marketing survey, "but first—we'll have to take time out for a commercial." Stand with your eyes closed and silently count to twenty. Then open your eyes and explain that he didn't see it or hear it because it was a silent and invisible commercial—"in my mind—and perhaps it is now in your mind, too. . . ."

Remove the bunch of four different tags from your "ticket pocket." Show him what is on them, give them to him, and ask him to read each of the names aloud. Take them back, stack them together in your right hand, and show them again. Turn your body a little to the left so everyone can see, and openly drop them into the right-hand pocket of your jacket—but really into the "ticket pocket" at the top of it.

Don't put your hand all the way into your pocket. Just spread the "ticket pocket" with the backs of your fingers, let the tags fall into it, and immediately remove your hand. This should be done with seeming carelessness, not as though you are being cautious about where they go.

Explain that your "sponsor" is the manufacturer of one of the four brands and that the survey is to test "whether silent commercials work," whether he will reach for one brand instead of the others "by some blind impulse." This is said to give a reason for having him choose blindly from your pocket, instead of simply looking at them and choosing one.

Without deliberately showing that your right hand is empty, let it be seen that it is. Put that hand just far enough into the top of your right-hand pocket so your fingers cover the "ticket pocket." Hook your left thumb into the top of the whole pocket at the opposite side, the side toward the spectator, and spread the pocket wide.

Hold it open that way as you shake it, as though mixing the tags that rattle in the bottom of it, and say, "Just dip your hand into my pocket and take one of them. Mix them up. Don't take the first one you touch—unless you want to. But take just one—any one—and bring it out."

As soon as he takes one, remove both your hands from the pocket. Ask him to read aloud the name on the tag he has "chosen." Repeat it. Then say: "You have had a note in your pocket since we began this survey. Will you open it now, please, and read it to everyone?"

He reads your thanks for listening to your silent commercial and the prediction that he would choose "Toasties."

Telepathy à la Carte

How it looks:

"Have you ever been in a restaurant where you just couldn't get the attention of the waiter and had to sit for what seemed hours before he finally took your order?" you ask. "Someday perhaps we'll solve the problem—by telepathy. Can you imagine a restaurant with a cook who's a mind reader? As soon as the patron reads the menu, they know in the kitchen exactly what he wants for dinner."

A spectator is asked to imagine himself in such a restaurant and is given a menu to look over so he can mentally decide what he would like to eat—appetizer, main course, dessert. When he has made up his mind about each, you ask him to write his choices on a slip of paper while you turn your head away, and to fold the slip and give it to another spectator "so we can check your order later if there's any question."

You read aloud the menu list of appetizers, ask the first spectator to concentrate on the one he has in mind, and you reveal what it is. Then you announce what he has chosen as the main course of his imaginary dinner. But when you come to the dessert, you find that you can't read his thoughts—so you turn to the other spectator, who has been holding the written slip, and read his mind instead.

What you need:

A 9-by-6-inch piece of *white* transfer paper, the kind sold at sewing counters for tracing dress patterns.

A 9-by-12-inch sheet of black construction paper.

Several slips of thin paper from a small scratch pad.

A hard lead pencil with a freshly sharpened point.

A paper clip.

The use of a typewriter.

The secret and setup:

The white transfer paper serves the purpose of carbon paper, but it doesn't look like carbon paper. The menu is typed on it, and its innocent appearance permits it to be openly displayed inside a black menu cover, which contains nothing but that typed menu. When the spectator is given a slip of paper to write down his mental choices, he rests it on the menu cover, and a faint white impression of the writing is transferred to the inside black cover so that later you can secretly read it as you consult the menu.

The menu cover is simply made by folding the sheet of black construction paper as you would close a book. Put the paper lengthwise on a table, bring the left side over to the right until those two edges exactly meet, and crease the center fold.

At the top of the *shiny* side of the white transfer paper, type the word: MENU. Space down a few lines and type the heading: APPETIZERS. List several choices, but keep them short and simple, such as Tomato Juice, Fruit Cup, Melon. Avoid unusual foods, foreign spellings, anything that would be difficult for the spectator to remember or to write.

Under the next heading, MAIN COURSE, list such plain things as Steak, Chops, Roast Beef, Shrimps, Fish. Under the DESSERT heading you might list Pie, Ice Cream, Cake. Don't be tempted to add other courses—three choices will be enough for the spectator to keep in mind.

Paper-clip the top of the menu to the *left* inside cover of the black folder and have it on your table with the slips of paper and pencil.

What you do:

After you have invited the spectator to imagine himself in a restaurant where telepathy is used, display the menu, hand it to him, and ask him to choose what he would like to start the meal, then his main course, and then dessert. "Keep the choices in your mind," you say. "Appetizer, main course, and dessert." Walk back to your table as you give him time to make his mental selections, pick up a slip of paper and the pencil, and return to him again. "When you have done that, just close the menu."

As he closes it, you should be right beside him to hand him the pencil and to place the slip of paper on the front of the folded menu cover. "Now please write down your order so

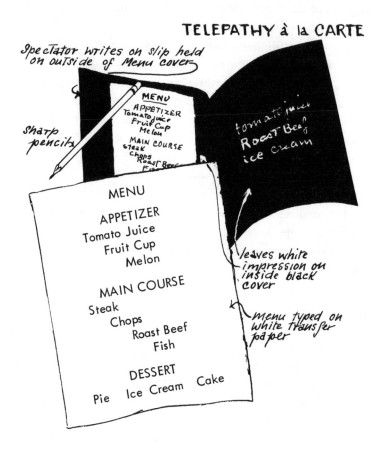

TELEPATHY à la CARTE

Spectator writes on slip held
on outside of Menu cover

MENU
APPETIZER
Tomato Juice
Fruit Cup
Melon
MAIN COURSE
Steak
Chops
Roast Beef
Fish

Sharp
pencils

tomato juice
Roast Beef
ice cream

MENU

APPETIZER
Tomato Juice
Fruit Cup
Melon

MAIN COURSE
Steak
Chops
Roast Beef
Fish

DESSERT
Pie   Ice Cream   Cake

leaves white
impression on
inside black
cover

menu typed on
white transfer
paper

we can check it later if there's any question." Hold the slip of paper on the cover so he can take it and then immediately turn away.

When he has written his choices on the slip, you say, "I'll ask you to fold it, please, and give it to that lady next to you." Look at the second spectator and ask, "Will you be kind enough to keep it for us?"

Take the menu from the first spectator, casually tuck it under your arm, and move well away from him. "I get the impression that you're a man who really enjoys his food," you say. "You're not on a diet, are you?—I hope not. Anyhow, you don't have to worry about calories. This is strictly a mental meal. I guarantee you won't gain a pound."

Open the menu and start to read aloud from the list of appetizers, enlarging a bit on the simple typed descriptions. "You might have chosen the Tomato Juice Cocktail, the California Fresh Fruit Cup, or the Iced Persian Melon to start your meal. Then, for a main course . . ."

As you continue to read the possible menu choices, glance to the right of the inside cover; there the "carbon" impression of what he wrote on the paper slip will appear in white against the black. Depending on the lighting in the room, you may have to tilt the menu a little so the impression shows clearly. This is a matter of moving the cover very slightly until it catches the light at the right angle.

Memorize the three choices and toss the menu on your table as you begin to reveal his thoughts. "You decided to start with Tomato Juice," you might say, "and then you mentally ordered the Prime Roast of Beef. . . . That was rare, wasn't it—or do you prefer it well done?" Look at him and ask, "Have I been right so far—Tomato Juice, Roast Beef?" Wait for him to say so, then say, "And now, what for dessert?"

Pretend to be having difficulty. Finally admit that you can't get his thoughts clearly. Turn to the other spectator who has been holding the written slip and say, "I'm afraid I'll have to read your mind instead. Will you please look at the slip of paper you have and concentrate on what he wants for dessert?"

Then announce, for instance: "Oh, of course — Ice Cream. I thought first of chocolate — chocolate cake. But it is Ice Cream." Look at the first spectator and ask, "Is that correct? Did I get your order exactly right? Tomato Juice — Roast Beef — Ice Cream?"

5

Mental Visions

Toll the Hour

How it looks:

You take an envelope from your pocket and remove a card from it, on which there is a drawing of a numbered clock dial without hands. One of a group of spectators gathered around a table is asked to think of something that happened to him yesterday or that will happen tomorrow.

"It could be something trivial or something important," you say, giving him a pencil. "I want you to think of the hour of that happening—never mind the minutes—and draw in a hand to that hour on this clock. Just draw a straight line—an arrow—from the center of the dial to the hour."

While he is doing that, you turn your head so you can't see, and then ask him to place the drawing facedown on the table. Facing the group again, you slide the card flatly across the table and put it into the envelope, which you seal. Both sides of the envelope are shown so there will be no doubt that the clock dial is entirely covered from view.

"Your thought of that hour exists in two dimensions—in your mind and in the physical expression of it on the drawing sealed in this envelope," you say. "If I were to tear up the drawing, the thought would be physically destroyed." You tear the envelope and the drawing inside it into small pieces and discard them by dropping them into your pocket. "In a strictly physical sense, the hour is now lost. But, of course, the thought of that hour still remains in your mind."

For a moment, you stand silent, and close your eyes. "In *my* mind," you say then, "I hear a clock tolling—chiming the hour." You slowly tap the end of the pencil on the table, sounding it one, two, three times. Opening your eyes, you tell the spectator: "The hour in your mind is three o'clock."

What you need:

A 2½-by-4¼-inch manila coin envelope with an end-opening flap. It should be of good quality paper, thick enough so it cannot be seen through.

A blank card, cut slightly smaller than the envelope.

Pencil, pen, and scissors.

The secret and setup:

Although the envelope is convincingly shown on both sides so it appears to have no openings, it does have a hole cut in the face of it. But the hole is so small that it can be covered by the ball of your thumb when the envelope is held in a way it normally would be held to display it. Through the hole you are able to see the center of the clock dial and enough of the "hand" that the spectator has drawn on it to tell the hour to which it points.

Start by drawing the clock dial on the card with the pen. In the center of the card, make a circle about 2¼ inches in diameter. The size need not be exact, but the dial should be large enough so the numbers will be well spaced around it. Number it from 1 to 12 as a clock is numbered, with the numbers positioned carefully where they would be on the face of a clock.

At the center of the circle make a fairly large dot. Then enlarge the dot just a bit more at the top, so the top of the dot points upward toward the 12. This is done so that when the numbers are covered by the envelope you can tell from looking at the point of the dot whether the dial is upside down.

With the scissors, cut a small "window" in the face of the envelope so that the dot of the clock dial will be at the center of this opening when the card is in the envelope. Cut it only in the face of the envelope, not through the back. The "window" should be about ½-inch-square so your thumb will cover it entirely. All you need to see is the bottom end of the line the spectator will draw, starting at the dot, to tell which hour the "hand" points to.

To understand how it is handled, have the envelope containing the card lengthwise and facedown on a table, flap end of the envelope to the right. Pick it up by bringing the tips of your right-hand fingers against the back of the envelope and sliding the envelope toward you off the edge of the table, where you naturally grip it by bringing your thumb up underneath. As you take the envelope, your thumb comes up right over the hole. You can feel the opening to make sure it is well covered.

Now turn your hand over from left to right and show the face of the envelope. With the "window" hidden by your covering thumb, the face looks as unprepared as the back. After you have shown it, turn your hand from right to left and drop the envelope on the table, facedown as before.

Later, when you take it again to tear it, you pick it up almost the same way, but with your hand more toward the right end of the envelope as you slide it back off the edge of the table and grip it from underneath with your thumb. That way your thumb does *not* cover the "window" and you can see the center of the clock dial through it as you hold up the envelope, its back toward the spectators.

Have the envelope, with the clock dial inside, in the right-hand pocket of your jacket and the pencil with it. The "window" face of the envelope should be toward your body.

What you do:

Reach into your pocket for the envelope. Feel for the "window," cover it with your thumb, and bring out the envelope. Casually show the face of it, turn it over, and drop it on the table with its back up.

Ask the spectator to think of something that happened or may happen to him, to think of the hour of that happening. Keeping the envelope flat on the table, open the flap and draw out the card. Show the clock dial on it and slide the card over to him. Take the pencil from your pocket.

"In a moment, I'll ask you to draw in a hand to that hour

on this clock—while I turn my head so that I can't see what hour you're thinking about." To demonstrate what you want him to do, you turn the pencil to its unpointed end so it won't make a mark and draw an imaginary straight line from the dot to one of the hours. "Just draw a straight line—an arrow—from the center of the dial to whatever hour you have in mind." You give him the pencil and turn your head away. "Have you done that? . . . Please turn the dial facedown on the table."

You face the group and slide the card over to the envelope. Open the flap and put the card in. Moisten the tip of your finger, wet the flap with it, and seal the envelope without lifting it from the table. Now pick up the envelope as previously explained, by sliding it toward you off the edge of the table so your thumb comes up underneath to take it and covers the hole.

Feel to make sure it is well covered, and then turn the envelope to show the face of it. Don't say anything about it, but give everybody a good chance to see it. Hold it that way a moment and then turn your hand over and drop the envelope facedown on the table.

"Your thought of that hour now exists in two dimensions— in your mind and in the physical expression of it on the drawing sealed in this envelope." You point to the envelope and slide it back off the edge of the table so that your thumb coming up to take it from beneath does *not* cover the hole.

Lift the envelope that way, with its face toward you and its back to the spectators, and glance through the "window" to see in which direction the dot at the center of the dial is pointed. If it points up, the dial is positioned correctly. But if the dot points down, the 12 on the dial is at the bottom. In that case, turn your hand and bring the point of the dot to the top.

Look at the spectator and say, "If I were to tear up the drawing, the thought would be physically destroyed." With

TOLL the HOUR

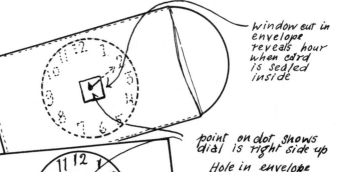

window cut in envelope reveals hour when card is sealed inside

point on dot shows dial is right side up

Hole in envelope covered with thumb

both hands, start to tear the envelope, and as you tear it look through the "window" to see where the clock "hand" is pointed. Imagine the clock dial and think around it—12, 3, 6, and so on—until you have mentally fixed the position of the pencil line at the right hour. Continue to tear the envelope to pieces, show the scraps in your hand, and drop them into your pocket.

"In a strictly physical sense, the hour is now lost," you say. "But, of course, the thought of that hour still remains in your mind."

Pick up the pencil the spectator has left on the table. Stand silent for a moment and close your eyes. Then say, "In *my* mind I hear a clock tolling—chiming the hour." Tap the pencil on the table to sound whatever the hour is. Open your eyes, look at the spectator, and tell him the hour that is in his mind.

Psychic Fingerprints

How it looks:

"May I have your autograph?" you ask a spectator as you give him a pen and a small card on which to write his name. "When you have written it, will you please put the card in this envelope and drop it on the table. I have a special reason for not touching that card again myself."

You then show two other cards and explain: "On one of these I have written the name 'George Washington' and on the other one 'Abraham Lincoln.' But the only genuine signature is the one you have just written. That would be obvious to anyone who could examine the writing. But with the cards hidden in envelopes it becomes impossible to see the writing, to identify yours from the others." You put your two cards in two similar envelopes and drop them to the table next to his.

"When you handled that card," you continue, "you gave me more than just your signature. You left your fingerprints all

over it. Not visible fingerprints, but the touch of your fingers—
what psychometrists might call the impression of your personality on the object you handled—psychic fingerprints. . . .
Please put all the envelopes in your pocket—and then remove
any one of them and hold it out before you."

He takes one of the envelopes from his pocket. Without
touching it you hold your hand above it, as if sensing the
vibrations. "No," you may say, "that's not yours. Try another
one, please." He removes them from his pocket, one at a time,
and when he holds the envelope containing the card he has
signed, you are able to tell him so. "Yes. That's the one that
bears your touch. Will you please open it and see if your
signature is on the card?"

You offer to try another experiment and ask him to put the
card back into the envelope and then to put all three envelopes
into his pocket again. "I want you to mix them up, shift them
around inside your pocket, until you are satisfied neither of
us could guess which is which," you say. "Now remove two of
the envelopes and toss them on the table—so there is just
one left in your pocket. It could contain the card with your
signature, or it could be one of the others."

Without touching the two envelopes he has tossed on the
table, you hold your hand over each in turn and then close to
the outside of his pocket. You then reveal which of the three
envelopes, whether on the table or in his pocket, contains the
card with his signature and have him open it to confirm your
discovery.

"Psychometry might explain that much," you say. "But it
doesn't explain what I will try to do now—because you
haven't touched the other cards at all, not since I put them

into their envelopes. There are no psychic fingerprints of yours on those." You point to one of the envelopes on the table and announce: "On the card in that envelope, you will find the name of George Washington. And on the one still in your pocket, the name of Abraham Lincoln."

You ask him to open each of the envelopes and read aloud the names, which prove to be exactly as you called them.

What you need:

Three 2½-by-4¼-inch manila coin envelopes with end-opening flaps, made of paper thick enough so there is no suspicion that writing can show through.

Three blank cards that will fit easily into the envelopes.

A pen and a rubber band.

The secret and setup:

The envelope into which the spectator puts his signature card is not marked in any way, but the other two are prepared so you can identify each of them at a glance no matter how they are held or tossed on the table. One is slightly creased at the sides and the other has its corners bent. These markings appear accidental, as if caused by handling the envelopes, and the routine centers the spectator's attention on the unmarked envelope.

To prepare the envelopes hold one at the bottom between your thumb and finger and strike the side edge of it sharply against the edge of a table. Tap it hard to leave an "accidental" crease and then smooth it out a little with your fingers. Do the same thing with the opposite side edge of that envelope. Take a second envelope and strike one of its bottom corners sharply on the top of a table so that the corner is bent, and then do the same with the opposite bottom corner.

Write the name "George Washington" on one of the cards and "Abraham Lincoln" on another. Then stack the cards and envelopes so the one with the creased sides is at the bottom, the one with bent corners next, then the "Washington" card, the "Lincoln" card, the third envelope, and the blank card on top. Put the rubber band around them and have them in one of your pockets with the pen.

What you do:

Take out the stack of cards and envelopes and remove the rubber band. Give the spectator the blank card and pen so he can write his signature. Hand him the plain envelope, ask him to put his signature card into it and to drop the envelope on the table. Say, "I have a special reason for not touching that card again myself."

Show him the "Lincoln" and "Washington" cards. Put the "Lincoln" card into the next envelope with the bent corners, then put the "Washington" card into the last envelope with the creased sides. Drop those to the table next to his. Point out that it is impossible to see the writing on the cards and identify his signature, then have him put all three envelopes in his pocket.

Ask him to take out any one. Hold your hand above it and pretend to sense the vibrations. Glance at the side edges and corners. If there is no crease or bend, you know the envelope is his.

If the first one he takes from his pocket isn't his, tell him so and have him drop that to the table and remove another. By glancing at it you will know whether that is it or whether the signature card is in the one still in his pocket. Reveal which one it is and have him open that envelope to confirm that you are right.

Ask him to put his signature card back into its envelope and put all three in his pocket again. Have him take out any two and toss them on the table. Once more, you discover where the correct envelope is and have him open it and verify his signature.

At this point, after his signature card has been eliminated, there may be two envelopes on the table, or only one on the table and one still in his pocket. In either case you know which is which and where each of them is. All you have to remember is that the envelope with bent corners has the "Lincoln" card in it and the one with creased sides contains the "Washington" card. If "Lincoln" is on the table, for example, then "Washington" must be in his pocket.

Announce that you are going to carry the experiment beyond what might be explained by psychometry or "psychic fingerprints." Then point in turn to each card on the table, or one on the table and one in his pocket, and say: "On the card in that envelope you will find the name of George Washington. . . . And on this one—Abraham Lincoln."

The Bagged Bill

How it looks:

You ask if someone will please take out a dollar bill and hold it up. "Fold it in half so George Washington is on the inside—and then fold it a couple of times more," you say. "You'll remember that George Washington never told a lie . . . so I might as well admit the truth. What I really want—is to borrow your dollar for a few moments, if you'll be kind enough to bring it up to me. But keep it tightly folded that way, please."

Taking the folded bill between your thumb and finger, you hold your hand up high. With your other hand you pick up a paper bag, shake it open, and drop it upside down over the hand holding the bill, so that the bag completely covers your hand and part of your upheld arm.

You give the spectator a slate and chalk. "What I'm going to attempt to do is read the serial numbers on your dollar bill," you explain, "but with my mind instead of my eyes. As I call out the numbers, will you write them on the slate—large enough for everyone to see?"

With some hesitation, and a mistake or two that you correct, you call out the numbers. You remove the paper bag that covers your hand, crumple up the bag with your free hand and toss it aside, and return the still-folded bill to the spectator, as you take the slate and chalk from him.

"Open your dollar and check the numbers with me, please," you say, "to see how close I came. Read them slowly, so we can check each number."

As he reads the serial numbers from his bill, you point to each digit on the slate, and then make a large check mark as the total number proves to be entirely correct.

What you need:

A dollar bill that is in average condition, neither crisply new nor badly worn.

A flat-bottomed brown paper grocery bag, about 4-by-7-by-13 inches when opened out.

A slate, about 8-by-12 inches.

Chalk and a pencil.

Double-faced (sticky both sides) transparent tape.

The secret and setup:

The paper bag, which apparently serves to keep you from seeing the bill in your hand, also allows you to switch the borrowed bill for one of your own with serial numbers that have been copied on the side of the bag in advance.

Your own folded dollar with its known numbers is stuck to a piece of tape inside the bag at the start. With your hand inside the bag you switch it for the borrowed one. At the end, when you pull the bag off your hand, you pinch the borrowed bill in one corner of it and it stays hidden in the bag as you crumple up the bag and toss it aside on your table. You are left holding your own bill, which looks like the still-folded bill the spectator gave you. He opens that one to read the numbers you have called as you check them off on the slate.

Open out the bag and put it on a table with its mouth towards you. On the left side panel, right at the mouth of the bag, print the serial numbers of your dollar bill with the pencil. Keep the bag in the same position and fasten a short strip of double-faced tape *inside* that left side panel about an inch from the bottom of the bag.

Turn the dollar bill lengthwise with Washington's picture face up and fold it in half from left to right, again in half, and then from top to bottom. Stick the folded bill to the tape inside the bag. Close the bag flat and have it on top of the slate and chalk on your table, with the mouth of the bag to the rear.

What you do:

Ask if someone will please take out a dollar bill and hold it up. If several spectators hold up bills, try to choose one that nearly matches the condition of your own bill that is hidden inside the bag, neither brand new nor badly worn. In any case, hurry things along so the person won't have much chance to examine it carefully. Tell him to fold the bill "so George Washington is on the inside" and then to fold it a couple of times more. By wording the instructions that way, you avoid saying anything about the serial number that might cause him to look at it before he folds the bill.

Have him bring it to you. Stand at the right of the table with the spectator to your right. Take the bill from him with the thumb and finger of your right hand. If he hasn't folded it enough, give it another fold so it somewhat matches the bill hidden in the bag. Then hold that hand high, with your arm outstretched and your fingers open wide so it can be plainly seen that there is nothing else in your hand.

With your left hand take the bag from the table. Shake it open, turn it upside down, and pull it down over your upheld right hand to cover it with the bag. Keep your left hand at the mouth of the bag a moment, as if adjusting it, but really to hold the bag so it won't twist around.

With your right hand up inside the bag pull your bill from the sticky tape. Just scoop it off the tape with your free fingers and close them around it. The borrowed bill remains held between your thumb and first finger, as it was, with your own bill closed in your other fingers to keep the two apart.

Drop your left hand to your side. Turn your right arm around slowly to show all sides of the bag so it can be seen—

without your saying so—that there are no holes or slits of any
kind in it. Then bring your hand back to its original position
and keep it held up that way with the bag upside down over it.

Take the chalk and then the slate from the table with your
left hand. "What I'm going to attempt to do," you say, "is to

The BAGGED BILL

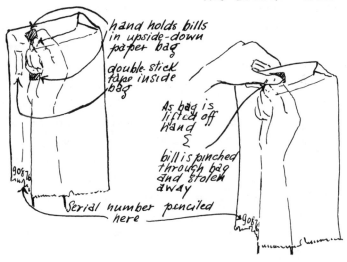

hand holds bills
in upside-down
paper bag

double-stick
tape inside
bag

As bag is
lifted off
hand

bill is pinched
through bag
and stolen
away

Serial number penciled
here

read the serial numbers of your dollar bill—but with my mind
instead of my eyes." Give the chalk and slate to the spectator.
"As I call out the numbers, will you write them on the slate—
large enough for everyone to see?"

Glance at the numbers penciled at the mouth of the bag
and memorize the first few. Turn your head away, pretend to
concentrate, and call out two of the numbers. Then call a
wrong number and quickly correct yourself. "No—that's not
right. Make that a two—not a seven. Five, three, two . . . ."

Look at the spectator, as if to see if he is writing them correctly on the slate. Steal another glance at the penciled numbers on the bag. Turn your head away again and slowly call out the rest of the numbers.

When you have called all of them, bring your left hand to the top left corner of the bag to pull it off your right hand. Inside the bag, push the borrowed bill into that corner with your right fingers. Pinch it through the bag with your left first finger and thumb and lift the bag straight up off your right hand, taking the borrowed bill with it. As you do that, bring the other bill up to the tips of your right fingers so that hand can hold up what appears to be the still-folded bill borrowed from the spectator.

Crumple up the paper bag with your left hand and carelessly toss it aside on the table. Give the spectator the folded bill and take the slate and chalk from him. Tell him to open the dollar and to "check the numbers with me, please, to see how close I came—read them slowly, so we can check each number."

Hold the slate facing the audience and touch each digit with the chalk as he calls the number aloud. When he has called the whole number, read it off the slate again and make a big check mark. (And don't forget, after the show, to retrieve the other dollar from the crumpled paper bag.)

Crystal Vision

How it looks:

"Have you ever gazed into a crystal ball?" you ask a spectator. "No? Would you like to attempt to discover for us something that hasn't happened yet?" You pick up a drinking glass from your table. "I haven't brought along a crystal ball. But perhaps we can imagine this drinking glass is one."

Holding the glass on the outstretched palm of your hand, you slowly lift it into the spectator's direct line of vision. "I want you to think of some simple geometric figure — perhaps a circle, a triangle, a square. If you do imagine that you see anything, don't tell us what it is — not *what* you see. Just tell us whether you see any figure at all. . . . You do? There's an image in your thoughts?"

You snap your fingers and then hand the glass to the spectator. "Look into it now. Do you still see something? Nothing at all? Then the vision must have been entirely in your own mind. . . . But please remember what you think you saw. We'll both keep that thought a secret from everybody else for a moment."

Turning to a second spectator, you show him a series of geometric designs on a set of cards, which you display one at a time. "I want you to make an entirely random choice," you explain. "Nothing that could be a preconceived thought. I'll turn these so that you can't see their faces. As I hold each up, please just call out which one you want. Any one at all. . . . This one?"

Without showing the design he has chosen, you rest the card face down on top of the glass on your table. To the first spectator, you say, "A moment ago, you had a brief vision of something. Will you please tell everybody now what it was? When you did your crystal gazing, what figure did you see?"

He says: "A triangle."

"You saw it in your mind before the gentleman over there

made his choice," you say. "A mental vision of something that hadn't happened yet. . . ."

Lifting the card from the glass, you hold it to show that the design the second spectator chose was — a triangle.

"Congratulations," you say. "For a first try as a crystal gazer — I think you deserve our applause."

What you need:

A clear, straight-sided drinking glass.

White transfer paper, the kind sold at sewing counters for tracing dress patterns.

Fifteen 4-by-8-inch blank index file cards.

A ball-point pen and a broad-tipped black marking pen.

Transparent tape.

A pair of scissors.

A rubber band.

The secret and setup:

A white transfer paper impression of a tiny triangle is marked on the side of the glass ahead of time. This sort of paper leaves a waxy mark that can be erased with a quick rub of the thumb, so that when the spectator looks into the glass a second time there is nothing to see. The stack of design cards shown to the other spectator includes six duplicate triangles and they are stacked so he is forced to choose one of those.

Wash the glass and dry it thoroughly. Cut a 1-inch square from the white transfer paper. Stick the waxy side of it firmly to the side of the glass, about halfway down from the top, with small tabs of tape. Draw a triangle on it with the ball-point pen, pressing hard so the design will transfer to the glass.

Leave the square of transfer paper taped to the glass until you are ready to use it, to avoid smudging the design. The glass can be carried that way in a briefcase with other props.

Turn the file cards with their narrow edges at the top and bottom. With the black marking pen, making the designs as large as will neatly fit, draw a triangle on seven of the cards, a circle on two of them, then a cross, a square, a rectangle, an oval, a right angle, and a star.

Stack the cards *faceup* in this order: Put six of the triangles together, one of the circles on top of those, then the cross, square, rectangle, the seventh triangle, the oval, right angle, star, and finally the second circle. Fasten the rubber band around them to keep them in proper sequence.

To set things up for performance remove the taped paper from the glass and place the glass on your table with the waxed triangle design to the rear. Have the design cards beside it.

What you do:

Have the first spectator stand at the left of your table while you stand in front of the table facing him. Pick up the glass by its top rim with your left hand and rest the bottom of it on your outstretched right palm. Raise it until you have brought the glass level with the spectator's eyes. At this point, the design is at the rear of the glass, so the spectator will see nothing as he looks through the sides of it.

Tell him to concentrate on the glass as if it were a crystal ball and to think of some simple geometric figure—"perhaps a circle, a triangle, a square." But caution him not to reveal what he sees. Say: "If you do imagine that you see anything, don't tell us what it is — not *what* you see. Just tell us whether you see any figure at all — not what that particular figure may be. Do you understand?"

As you speak, slowly turn your outstretched hand to revolve the direction of the glass a half-turn so as to bring the side with the waxed design toward yourself. This brings the little triangle directly into the spectator's line of vision as he looks through his side of the glass. Ask: "Are your thoughts begin-

CRYSTAL VISION

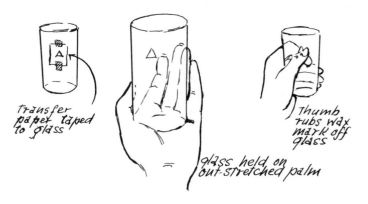

Transfer paper taped to glass

glass held on out-stretched palm

Thumb rubs wax mark off glass

ning to form around some image that is becoming vivid in your mind? . . . Don't describe it yet. You do see something? There's a clear image of some figure in your thoughts?"

As soon as he says that he sees what it is, bring your left hand up to the glass so that your thumb comes right over the waxed mark, and lift the glass away with that hand. There's no need to hurry the action. Look at the glass yourself as you talk and just bring your thumb over the design as your left hand picks up the glass from your right palm.

Drop your left hand to your side, carrying the glass with it, and secretly rub your thumb across the side of the glass to erase the design. This takes only a sweep of your thumb. At the same time, raise your right hand and snap your fingers, as if to clear the spectator's mind of his "vision."

"Look into it now," you say, as you hand him the glass. "Do you still see something?" Give him time to look over the glass, on which he will find no trace of the triangle he saw. "Nothing at all? Then the vision must have been entirely in your own mind. But please remember what you think you saw. We'll both keep that thought a secret from everybody else for a moment."

Take the glass from him, put it on your table, and pick up the design cards. Point to a second spectator in the audience and ask, "Will you please join in our experiment, sir? . . . There's no need to leave your seat. I just want you to look at these symbols that I have." Remove the rubber band and hold the stack of cards facing the audience, with the first circle design showing at the front.

Point to that front card and say, "A circle." Remove it and put it at the back of the stack behind all the others. Point to the next card and say, "A star." Put that at the back and continue showing them that way and calling out what each design is until you come to the second circle card. Say, "The circle again—which brings us back to where we started."

Leave that where it is at the face of the stack. Turn the whole stack around so the backs of the cards are toward the spectator and the circle card faces you. "I'll turn these so that you can't see their faces," you explain, "because I want you to make an entirely random choice of one of these symbols—nothing that could be a preconceived thought."

Lift off the circle card, keeping its back to him, and hold it up to demonstrate as you say, "I'll hold them up one at a time and I want you to call out—whenever you want me to stop. Choose any one you wish." Put that behind the rest of the stack. The first of the six duplicate triangle cards now faces you. Hold it up, with its back to him, and ask, "This one?" Put that at the back of the stack, take the next triangle, hold it up back outwards the same way, and ask, "This?"

Continue until he calls out to choose one. Without showing it rest it face down on top of the glass on your table and put the other cards aside. Turn to the first spectator and say, "A moment ago, you looked into this glass and had a brief vision of something. When you did your crystal gazing you saw some figure—some design. . . . Will you please tell everybody now what it was that you saw?"

He says: "A triangle."

"You saw it in your mind before the gentleman over there made his choice." Lifting the card from the top of the glass, you hold it to show the triangle. "A mental vision of something that hadn't happened yet. . . . Congratulations. For a first try as a crystal gazer—I think you deserve our applause."

Comic Strip Clairvoyance

How it looks:

"I've clipped a bunch of comic strips out of the newspapers," you say, holding up a batch of them. "All your favorite funny characters—and mine. Different papers,

different strips, different days." You show them to one of the
spectators as you read off some of the names. "Plain Jane,
Momma, Broom Hilda, Steve Roper, Judge Parker, Rex
Morgan. . . ."

Turning them all facedown, you give him some, invite him
to choose one of them, but caution him not to let you see it.
You also give him a small envelope. "I want you to read that
comic strip to yourself," you explain. "Read the name printed
at the top and think about the character and the events that
are pictured. Then please fold it up, put it into the envelope,
and seal it."

While he is doing that, you go to two other spectators,
have them choose comic strips and give them envelopes to
seal them in. You then collect the three envelopes, put them
into your pocket, and return to the front of the room.

"I have no way of knowing which comic strip each of you
chose to put into the sealed envelopes that are still in my
pocket," you say. "But in my mind the characters I see most
clearly are—Li'l Abner . . . Mutt and Jeff . . . Andy Capp.
If I have correctly named the comic strip any of you is thinking about—will you please hold up your hand?"

You look at the three spectators, all of whom have raised
their hands. "All three of you? All three correct. . . . I am
getting your thoughts clearly. Let's see if I can get any of the
pictures in your minds."

Removing one of the sealed envelopes from your pocket,
you hold it to your forehead and describe the events that are
pictured on the comic strip sealed within it. Repeat this pro-
cedure with the second and third envelopes, each in turn.
Once more, you ask the three spectators: "If I have correctly

described the pictures that were in your minds — any of you — will you hold up your hands?"

Again all three hold up their hands. "All three," you say. "Thank you. That is unusual."

What you need:

Three duplicate copies of the same issue of a daily newspaper that contains a page of comic strips. These should be full comic strips, each with several panels of pictures, not single-frame cartoons. They should be black and white, not Sunday color comics, with plain newsprint on the back of them.

A few newspapers with different comic strips, to provide a variety.

Six 2½-by-4¼-inch manila coin envelopes with end-opening flaps.

A pair of scissors.

A pen or pencil.

A rubber band.

The secret and setup:

Although a lot of different strips are shown, all three spectators are limited to choosing one from identical sets of three strips. It doesn't matter which of those three they choose, or if they all happen to choose the same strip, since you reveal all three possibilities before you ask whether theirs was among the three you named.

The same principle applies when you reveal the details of what is pictured in the strips. You don't know or care who chose what or which envelope he put it in — it has to be among the three you describe—and none of the three spectators knows which strip any other spectator chose.

You are able to describe the strips in some detail without having to memorize them because the information is written on the faces of three dummy envelopes that you take from your pocket instead of the sealed envelopes that you had put there. As you hold the envelopes before your eyes, you just read what is secretly written on them.

Start by deciding which three comic strips you intend to have the spectators select. Cut those out of the duplicate newspapers and make up three sets, each of which contains all three strips. Put those three sets aside for a moment. Now cut a batch of different comic strips from the various newspapers, so that altogether you have about twenty, with different names and characters.

Put one of the envelopes lengthwise and faceup on a table, with its flap end to the left. On the face of that envelope, print a brief description of one of the three comic strips you have chosen for the duplicate sets. The information should be printed at the center of the envelope in several short lines. You might print, for example: MUTT-JEFF/ JEFF PLAYING CARDS/ GETS HOME 2 A.M./ WIFE WAITS WITH ROLLING PIN/ JEFF SAYS: "DON'T TELL ME YOU'RE UP THIS LATE BAKING A CAKE."

Write similar short descriptions on the faces of two more envelopes for the other two strips. Then take any three *different* comic strips, not strips from your duplicate sets, and fold them up. Put one of those into each of the three envelopes on which you have written descriptions and seal them. That is done to give the dummy envelopes the appearance of having comic strips sealed inside them so the envelopes will have some bulk.

Lay the three sets of duplicate strips *faceup* on a table. Put the rest of the different strips faceup on top of those. Fold all the strips together into a small bundle and fasten the rubber band around them.

Have the bundle of comic strips in the right-hand pocket of your jacket, along with the three empty unsealed envelopes. The three dummy envelopes go into your left-hand pocket. Stand them stacked together on end, flap ends at the top, with their written faces toward your body.

What you do:

Take out the bundle of comic strips, remove and discard the rubber band, and open them out full length. Display them and explain what they are and hold them faceup in your left hand. Show them to one of the spectators by thumbing them off one at a time into your right hand, as if you were counting dollar bills from hand to hand. Read aloud the names of the strips as you show them. When you have shown the spectator about a dozen, put them all back on *top* of the stack in your left hand.

"I'll turn them all over so we don't know which is which," you say. Turn the whole stack over together with your right hand so they lie facedown in your left hand. The first identical set of three preselected strips is now facedown on top of the stack. "Will you please take some?" You don't say how many, but just count off three and give them to the spectator. "Keep them turned down so I can't see them. Mix them up if you like. You have a free choice. Please choose one of them — any one you wish — and then give me back the rest."

Hold out your right hand to take the two he returns and put those at the *bottom* of the whole stack in your left hand. Say: "I want you to read the comic strip you have chosen. Read it to yourself. Read the name printed at the top of the strip and think about the characters and the events that are pictured. Then please fold it up and seal it in this envelope." Take one of the empty envelopes from your right-hand pocket and give it to him. "While you're doing that, I'll give some of the other comic strips to somebody else."

The second set of preselected strips is now facedown on top of the stack. Go to a second spectator who is at some distance from the first one. As you approach him, count three strips off the stack and give them to him as you say: "Will you take some, please, and hold them so I can't see them — keep them turned down. Then choose one and give me back the others."

Again, put the two that he returns on the *bottom* of the stack, which leaves the next preselected set on top. Instruct him to read his chosen strip to himself, as you did the first spectator, and hand him an envelope to seal the strip in after he has read it. Move on to a third spectator, who isn't too close to the second, and repeat the same thing.

Collect the three envelopes and as you take each one say, loudly enough for the whole audience to hear, "Thank you. I'll put it in my pocket." Openly put them into your left-hand pocket, but lengthwise, so that they don't mix with the three dummy envelopes that are endwise in that pocket. Return to the front of the room.

"I have no way of knowing which comic strip each of you chose to put into the sealed envelopes that are still in my pocket," you say. "But the characters I see most clearly in my mind are . . ." Call out the names of the three you have pre-selected, for example, "Li'l Abner . . . Mutt and Jeff . . . Andy Capp." Look quickly from the first spectator to the second and third. "If I have correctly named the one any of you is thinking about—will you please hold up your hand?" Wait for the audience to realize that three hands are raised. "All three of you? I am getting your thoughts clearly. Let's see if I can get any of the pictures in your minds."

With your left hand take one of the dummy envelopes from your pocket, holding the top end of it between your thumb and first finger. Being careful not to turn it, bring it straight up against your forehead and keep it there a moment. Then lower it a little so it is in front of your eyes and you can read the writing on it. When you have read enough to have the information fixed in mind, bring the envelope straight down against your chest, still without turning it, and hold it there as you describe what is pictured in one of the comic strips.

Take that envelope with your right hand and put it away in your right-hand pocket. With your left hand remove another envelope from the pocket on that side and bring it up in front of you to secretly read what is on it. Then put that away in your right-hand pocket. When you have described all three comic strips, say: "If I have correctly described the pictures that were in your minds—any of you— will you hold up your hands?"

Wait for all three to raise their hands as before. Then say: "All three of you again. Thank you. That is unusual."

Double Image

How it looks:

"I want you to picture something in your mind—not a word or a number, but a visual image of some simple object or design," you say to a spectator. "It could be a face . . . ." With a piece of chalk you draw a face on a slate and erase it. "Or it might be a geometrical figure such as a square with a circle inside it." You draw that to show him, then erase it and give him the slate and chalk. "Will you stand facing me, please, and hold the slate so I can't see what you draw— with your back to the others so that they *can* see?"

He faces you with his back to the audience and draws on the slate. When he has finished drawing, you say, "I'll put it into this envelope to cover it." You take the slate from him at arm's length, and without looking at it you keep it upright and slide it into a large envelope. Fastening the flap shut, you show both sides of the envelope. "Please think about what you have drawn—picture it again in your mind."

Holding the envelope, the slate sealed inside it, you take a black crayon and begin to draw on its face. "Please understand that I won't attempt to duplicate exactly what you have in mind," you explain. "I'm certainly no artist, and, as I said, we're dealing not with words or numbers but with a mere image of something. I can only draw whatever I may see in my own mind. . . . What I do see is this. . . ."

You describe some features of it as you draw a sketch on the envelope. Then you turn the envelope so the audience can see what you have drawn. Unfastening the clasp, you remove the slate and hold the two side by side. Your drawing on the envelope roughly matches what the spectator drew on the slate.

What you need:

A piece of Silver Mylar, cut with scissors to a size about 5 inches long and 1¼ inches wide. This is thin paperlike metallic film with a silvered mirror finish, which is available at art supply stores. It is manufactured in rolls and usually sold by the yard.

A wooden-framed "school" slate, about 8-inches-square.

White chalk.

A few facial tissues.

A 9-by-12-inch manila clasp envelope of good quality paper that cannot be seen through.

A dark black wax crayon.

Double-faced (sticky both sides) transparent tape.

The secret and setup:

The Silver Mylar strip is fastened to the inside of the envelope flap where it serves as a mirror so that you can see a clear reflection of the drawing as you slide the slate into the envelope. Being light in weight and with no bulk, it in no way interferes with the natural handling of the envelope, and it is entirely hidden from view when the envelope flap is closed.

Turn the envelope so the flap is at the top and attach the strip of Silver Mylar lengthwise to the inside of the flap, centered directly beneath the clasp hole. Attach it with double-faced tape, fastened to the back of the Mylar along its top and bottom edges. The long bottom edge of the mirrored strip should just clear the fold, so the flap can be opened and closed easily.

To see how it works make a simple drawing on the slate with the chalk. Stand the slate on end, upright against some-

DOUBLE IMAGE

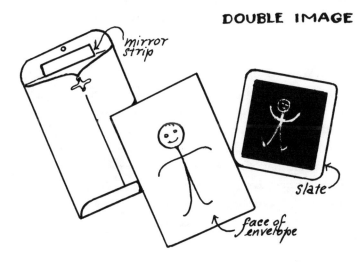

thing on top of a bookcase with the drawing faced away from you. Take the envelope with its back toward you and unfasten the flap. Bring your left hand to the top of the opened flap, thumb at the rear and fingers in front, and hold the envelope that way so it hangs down from that hand.

Stand at arm's length from the slate and take it with your right hand, between your thumb and fingers at the top, keeping it faced away from you. Hold out the envelope with your left hand, lower it a little, and with your right hand *slowly* slide the slate down inside it. As you do that, tilt the flap out slightly—as you naturally would to insert the slate. By looking at the mirrored strip you will see a reflection of the drawing as the slate goes into the envelope.

To set things for performance, have the envelope on your table, back upward and with the flap fastened by the clasp. Put the slate, cleaning tissues, and chalk on top of the envelope and the black crayon in your right-hand pocket.

What you do:

Pick up the slate, chalk, and tissues. Explain to the spectator that you want him to picture something in his mind—"a visual image of some simple object or design." This is to plant the idea that it is the picture in his mind that is important, not the fact that he will draw it on a slate, and to suggest that it should be a simple and uncomplicated drawing.

"It could be a face. . . ." You draw just a circle with lines for eyes, nose, and mouth, again to stress that you want him to make a quick and simple sketch. "Or it might be a geometrical figure. . . ." You draw a plain square with a circle inside. Erase each drawing with a tissue. Then give him the slate and chalk and ask him to stand facing you with his back to the audience and to hold the slate so you can't see what he draws.

While he is drawing on the slate, turn to your table, pick up the envelope, casually show both sides of it, and tuck it under your left arm as you return to face the spectator. "Please tell me when you have finished," you say to hurry him a little. "Keep the back of the slate to me. . . . That's right." When he says he has finished, show both sides of the envelope again. Turn the back of it toward you, open the clasp, and lift the flap as you explain, "I'll put it into this envelope to cover it."

Hold the envelope with your left hand, as explained, between your thumb and fingers at the top of the flap so the envelope hangs down from that hand. Stand at arm's length from the spectator and take the slate from him with your right hand at the top of it. Slowly and deliberately, without turning the slate, insert the bottom end of its wooden frame into the envelope. Lower your left hand a bit for this and tilt the flap outward just a little. The weight of the slate going into the envelope makes tilting the flap almost automatic.

Look directly at the top of the envelope—as you naturally would to see that the slate goes into it properly. As you slowly slide the slate down past the flap, the drawing will be reflected in the mirrored strip. If you don't see it well enough at first glance, pull the slate back up a little, as if you were having slight difficulty getting it into the envelope, and steal another glance at the mirror, but don't overdo this. You don't have to remember every line of the drawing precisely, only enough to duplicate a rough sketch of it.

With both hands fold the flap shut and fasten the clasp. Take the envelope with your left hand at the left side of it, turn the envelope to show the audience the back of it again, and say to the spectator, "Please think about what you have drawn—picture it again in your mind." With your right hand remove the black crayon from your pocket.

Hold the envelope upright, face toward you so the audience can't see what you are drawing, and explain that you won't attempt to duplicate exactly what the spectator drew on the slate. Say: "I can only draw whatever I may see in my own mind. . . . What I do see is this. . . ." Then as you make your sketch, describe it in very general terms, as if you were trying to visualize the spectator's mental image.

If he pictured a simple sailboat, for instance, you might say: "I have an impression of an outdoor scene, a land-scape. . . . No, I'm wrong. It's a seascape—the ocean or a large lake, a great expanse of water. There's a boat sailing on the water. . . . Yes, a sailboat. . . ." This is partly to build the effect but also to keep the audience interested while you stand drawing something that they can't yet see.

When you have finished, turn the face of the envelope to show your sketch to the spectator and the audience and say, "I don't know how close that is. . . . The strongest picture in my mind was of a boat of some kind."

Open the envelope and leave the metal clasp squeezed open. Hold the envelope with your left hand and with your right hand pull the slate up out of the top of it. Put the slate in front of the envelope for a moment. Close the envelope flap and fasten the clasp. Then hold the envelope and the slate side by side, one in each hand, to compare your sketch with the picture from the spectator's mind.

6

I Predict

Some Predictions Do Come True

How it looks:

"For centuries there have been seers and soothsayers who claimed the ability to foretell the future by gazing into crystal balls, sifting sands through their fingers, reading cards and tea leaves," you say. "There is palmistry, numerology, and, of course, there is astrology. Whether it's by luck, coincidence, or whatever you want to believe—some predictions at times do seem to come true."

You show a spectator a number of metal-rimmed tags with strings attached. "Each tag has a different color," you explain. "Ten different colors. And on the other side each bears a number—from one to ten." After you have spread them out and he has had a chance to look them over, you ask him to select one. "You have an entirely free choice. Take them in your hands if you wish. Decide which one you will keep. All I ask is that once you have decided—don't change your mind."

He is requested to fasten his chosen tag by looping the string through a buttonhole of his jacket, "so it will remain in full view where everyone can see it." You then pick up a newspaper that has been lying on the table. "I've been reading the horoscope column in the paper," you say as you open it and fold it back to the proper page. "I don't know whether you believe in astrology or not, but these predictions are fun to read."

Handing him the paper, you ask if he will first look through the column for his astrological sign. "The birthdates are given there. Will you please read aloud what it says for you—just the part printed under your birthdate."

He reads his brief horoscope from the paper, and you say, "Whatever happens, please don't blame me for your horoscope. I didn't make the predictions printed in the paper. They aren't mine. . . . But if you'll look now at the bottom of the page, you'll see two lines written under all the rest, written with pen and ink. I did make those two predictions. I wrote them there. Will you read just the first one aloud?"

The spectator reads: "Your lucky color is green." You point to the color of the tag hanging from his jacket. "And it *was* green," you say. Turning the tag so he can read it, you ask, "What is the number on it?"

He answers: "Eight." You ask him to read aloud the next line from the newspaper and he reads: "Your lucky number is eight."

What you need:

Ten metal-rimmed white cardboard tags, 1¾ inch in diameter, with strings attached.

Ten copies of a newspaper that has a daily horoscope column. These may be ten different issues of newspapers that have been saved or ten copies all purchased at the same time. It makes no difference as long as they are the same size and each has a horoscope.

Paints or crayons in various colors.

A felt-tip black pen.

A small coin envelope in which to keep the tags.

The secret and setup:

The spectator's choice of a tag is entirely free, but the newspaper is prepared. It is made up of ten double pages, each of which includes a horoscope column, with a couple of other pages of any kind at the outside. Beneath each of the horoscope columns you write a prediction to match the color and number of one of the tags so that there are ten different predictions. You simply open the newspaper to the page with the prediction for the color and number of the chosen tag and have it read aloud.

These colors are suggested for the tags: white, blue, green, yellow, pink, red, orange, purple, brown, black. The white one is left plain, but on its back print a large number "1" with the black pen. Each of the others should be solidly colored on one side, and a large number should be printed on the reverse side in the same color. It makes no difference which number goes on what tag as long as they are numbered from one to ten.

From the ten newspapers remove all the double pages that include the horoscope column. Open out the first one on a table or on the floor so the horoscope faces you at either the left or right, wherever it happens to be printed in that issue. (You may have to turn the double page over to get the horoscope facing you.) Then put the next double page with a horoscope faceup on top of that, and so on with all the rest until you have stacked all ten. Close all the pages together, then take any other two or three double pages from one of the newspapers and put those at the outside around the others.

Open the prepared paper to the first horoscope page and at the top, where the page numbers are printed, write a small "1" with the pen. In the white margin at the bottom of that page print: YOUR LUCKY COLOR IS WHITE. Move down a space and print: YOUR LUCKY NUMBER IS 1.

Turn to the next horoscope page and at the top (left or right as the case may be) write a small "2." Take the tag numbered "2" and write the corresponding number and color predictions for that in the bottom margin. Continue to number and write predictions on each of the other horoscope pages in turn. When you have finished all ten, close the newspaper and fold it.

Stack all the tags together, straighten out their strings so they are not tangled, and slide them into the coin envelope. Have that on your table with the prepared newspaper.

What you do:

Make your opening remarks, invite a spectator to join you, and spill the tags out of the envelope to the table. Spread them out separately, hold up one or two by the strings so the audience can see what they are, and turn a few over as you explain: "Each tag has a different color. Ten different colors. And on the other side each bears a number — from one to ten."

You want both the spectator and the audience to be convinced that the tags are exactly as you say they are and that he does have a completely free choice. When he is satisfied and has chosen one, ask him to fasten it by the string to a buttonhole of his jacket so it will hang in full view, and help him to do that.

Take the newspaper, open it toward you, and as you make your comments about astrology, look for the page with a number at the top that matches the number of the tag he has chosen. Do this openly, as if you were going through the pages to find the one with a horoscope column. When you have the page you want, fold its opposite page and the rest back around behind the paper, then give it to the spectator as you point out the horoscope column to him.

He may notice the writing in the bottom margin, but you instruct him carefully. "First look through the column for your astrological sign," you say. "The birthdates are printed there. Will you please read aloud what it says for you — *just the part printed under your birthdate.*"

When he has read his brief printed horoscope from the

paper, you explain that you have written your own prediction "in pen and ink" at the bottom of the page. Point your finger to it and show him where you mean as you say, "I did make those two predictions. I wrote them there. Will you please read *just the first one* aloud?"

He reads it and you point to the tag hanging from his jacket. Take it by the edge and lift it with the color facing out for the audience to see. Say: "And it *was* green (or whatever the color is)" and then turn the tag so he can read the number and ask, "What is the number on it?" Repeat the number he says. Then ask him to read aloud your second prediction. Point your finger to it on the newspaper he is holding. He reads: "Your lucky number is eight" (or whatever it is).

Take the paper from him and toss it on the table. Thank him and say, "However you explain it—sometimes predictions do come true."

Let him keep the tag that is fastened to his jacket. You can easily make another one, and it is something that will encourage talk about your performance afterward when he shows it to his friends.

Symbolic Choice

How it looks:

You display three large cards, one with a red circle drawn on it, the second a square, and the third a triangle. Pointing to someone in the audience, you say: "Will you please look at each of these symbols intently for a moment without expressing any conscious thought?" After showing him each card separately, you turn to a second person in the audience and say: "Will you do the same thing, please? Just look at each of these. First the circle . . . now the square . . . and the triangle. Thank you."

"I'll make a record of my own thoughts," you explain as you take a pen from your pocket and write something on the back of one of the large cards without showing the audience what you write.

Facing the first spectator again, you say to him, "When I snap my fingers, will you please call out whichever one of these first comes to your mind — the circle, square, or triangle?" You snap your fingers and he says, perhaps, "The square."

You remove that card and prop it against a drinking glass at one side of your table. Then you ask the second spectator to choose one of the two remaining symbols in the same way, by calling out whichever one first comes to his mind when you snap your fingers. He may say, "The triangle." You remove that card and prop it against a glass at the other side of the table.

"The square . . . and the triangle," you say, pointing to each in turn. "And this is what I wrote before either choice was made. . . ." You show the audience the back of the one card still in your hand. On it you have written the words SQUARE AND TRIANGLE.

What you need:

Three 6-by-8-inch pieces of blank cardboard.
Two drinking glasses.

A red marking pen or crayon.

A black marking pen that can be clipped into your pocket.

The secret and setup:

Unknown to the audience, predictions have been written on the backs of two of the cards in advance. Because of the way they are held and handled, the backs of all three appear to be blank. The prediction you openly write on the back of the third card completes all the possible choices. Since two cards are removed by the successive choices, the pairing and elimination works out automatically, thus you are left at the end with the card that has the correct prediction on its back. That, of course, is the only prediction the audience ever sees.

With the red marking pen or crayon, draw a large circle on the face of one of the cards, a square on the second, and a triangle on the third.

Turn the "circle" card facedown. On its back, starting at a point about halfway down from the top and slightly to the right of center, print these words, one under another, with the black pen: SQUARE AND TRIANGLE. Make them large, but keep them to the lower right of the card and print the letters as you might have had you quickly jotted them down during the performance. Then draw a circle around the words.

In a similar position on the back of the "square" card, printed and circled in the same way, write: CIRCLE AND TRIANGLE. Leave the third card, the "triangle," blank on the back for now. That is the one on which you will openly write your prediction during the performance. When you do, it will be worded: CIRCLE AND SQUARE.

Stack the three together with their symbols faceup—the triangle at the bottom, then the square, and the circle on top. Turn them over with their backs to you and hold them upright, as though showing their faces to the audience. Now spread them in a fan so the backs overlap like a hand of play-

SYMBOLIC CHOICE

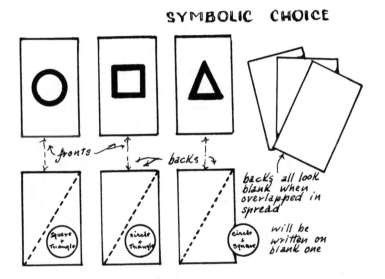

fronts   backs

backs all look blank when overlapped in spread

Square + Triangle

circle + Triangle

circle + Square   will be written on blank one

ing cards. You will see that you can spread them quite far without revealing the writing on the backs of the first two. Keep them in that overlapping spread and you can turn your hand around to show the apparently blank backs to the audience.

Nothing should suggest that the cards are being held in any special way to hide the fact that two of them already have predictions written on them. Just spread them casually, show the backs, then turn their faces to the audience and square them up again. When you display the faces separately, be careful to hold each card upright and close to you so nobody catches a glimpse of the writing on the back.

Have the cards properly stacked, faceup on your table, one drinking glass at each side of the table, and the black pen clipped into an inside pocket of your jacket.

What you do:

Pick up the cards, hold their backs toward you, and fan them out so the backs overlap to hide the writing. Turn them to casually show the backs and square them up again. Remove one card at a time to show the faces individually.

Choose someone in the audience, face the person, and say: "Will you please just look at each of these symbols intently for a moment, without expressing any conscious thought?" Show him the face of each card again. Then move over to a second spectator and ask that person to do the same thing. "Just look at each of these. First the circle . . . now the square . . . and the triangle."

After you show the three cards to the second spectator, square them together and pretend to concentrate for a moment as you explain, "I'll make a record of my own thoughts." Take out the black pen, casually turn the stack to show the back of the rear card, and turn them towards you again. Hold the stack up so nobody can see what you write, and on the back of that card, about where the predictions were written on the other ones, print and circle the words: CIRCLE AND SQUARE. Then mix the three cards, keeping their backs toward you.

Face the first spectator and ask him to please call out when

you snap your fingers whichever first comes to his mind—
the circle, square, or triangle. Repeat the name of whichever
he calls. Remove that card, its face still to the audience, and
stand it upright on the table with its back leaning against one
of the drinking glasses.

Go to the second spectator, show the two remaining symbols, and ask him to please call out when you snap your
fingers either of the two that are left—whichever one first
comes to his mind. When he calls it, remove whichever one
he names and prop that upright with its back against the
second glass on the table.

On the back of the one card still left in your hand is the
prediction that names the two that were chosen and removed.
Glance at the prediction, but don't reveal it yet. Point to each
of the cards standing on the table, and call out the names of
them *in the order in which the prediction is worded.* Finally, turn
the card that is in your hand around and hold it so the audience can see what you wrote "before either choice was
made."

To the Highest Bidder

How it looks:

Holding up a small package brightly gift-wrapped in red
tissue paper, you say: "Hours ago I put something in this
package. It could be something valuable—a watch, a set of
earrings, a ring, a pair of cufflinks. . . . And then again, it
could be worthless. I'm about to auction it off."

You put the package on your table and take a card and

pencil from your pocket as you explain, "I'll keep a record of your bids. Would anybody like to start things off? Come on, folks—for all you know this may be the opportunity of a lifetime. Isn't somebody willing to bid just one penny? . . . You, sir? Do I hear two? . . . The lady over there. I have two cents. Will somebody risk a whole nickel?" You raise the penny bidding as high as it will go. "I have sixteen cents then—is that all? Going once, going twice—gone for sixteen cents!"

When the final bid has been made, you write it on the card and put the pencil in your pocket. Shaking your head, you stare down at the card. "*Sixteen cents?* Sorry, lady—but I just won't sell it to you for that." You crumple up the card. "I refuse to accept your bid!" Then you smile. "Because if I took your money—I'd be cheating you. Instead, I'll give you what's inside the package absolutely free."

Taking the package from the table, you show it again and tear open the tissue paper. "You'll remember that I said I wrapped something in it hours ago? But all I put in the package was this price tag—the price of the highest bid." You remove a metal-rimmed price tag from the torn-open package and take it to the final bidder. "Will you please read it aloud—tell everybody what it says?"

She reads from the tag: "I predict that the highest bid will be . . . exactly sixteen cents."

What you need:

A round metal-rimmed cardboard tag, 1¾ inch in diameter, with its string removed.

A blank card about the size of a business card.

Red tissue paper and decorative tape of a contrasting color.

A pencil small enough to carry in a jacket pocket.

A pair of scissors.

The secret and setup:

There is nothing in the tissue paper package at the start. The card you hold in your hand as you write the bids has a hole in it and the tag is secretly held beneath it. When you write the final bid, you simply pencil in the amount on the tag itself, through the hole in the card. The card is crumpled up in order to dispose of it. Then you rest the package on the hand that holds the tag, tear through the tissue paper, and appear to take the tag from inside the package.

To prepare the card turn it with its narrow ends top and bottom, and about an inch up from the bottom cut a round hole approximately an inch in diameter.

Take the metal-rimmed tag and print on one side with the pencil, spacing out the words: I PREDICT THAT THE HIGHEST BID WILL BE . . . . After the last word draw an arrow that points to the other side. Turn the tag over and on the other side print the word EXACTLY right at the top, then leave the rest blank. Hold the top of the tag between your thumb and fingers and bend the metal rim outward very slightly to leave a small bump at the top. That is so you can tell which is the blank side by feeling the rim with your fingers later when the tag is in your pocket.

Use a piece of red tissue paper about 10 inches square to make up the dummy package. Keep folding it upon itself until you have a neat bundle about 3 inches square and then fasten it with a strip of decorative tape. Work the tissue with your fingers to pull out the sides and puff it into a shape that reasonably might contain some small item of value.

Put the pencil into the left-hand pocket of your jacket. Turn the tag so that its partly blank side faces you. Rest the card on top of the tag with the hole in the card to the bottom. Put them both into the same pocket with the pencil, the card lengthwise and the tag at the outside against the back of the card. They may shift around in your pocket before you get to use them, but that makes little difference since you can easily reposition them, as you reach into the pocket to take them out, by feeling for the bump in the tag's metal rim.

Have the dummy package on your table.

What you do:

Pick up the package and show it as you explain that hours ago you put something in it which might or might not be valuable and that you intend to auction it off. Place the package back on the table and leave it in plain view. Say that you will keep a record of the bids, then put your left hand into your jacket pocket as you ask if someone would care to start the bidding.

Inside your pocket feel for the little bump in the metal rim to reassure yourself that the partly blank side of the tag is still faced the right way in back of the card. With the tag toward the palm of your hand close your fingers around the card and pencil and bring them all out together.

Don't look at that hand or make any immediate attempt to adjust the position of the card and tag. Take the pencil with your right hand and let your left hand, the card and tag in it, drop to your side as you gesture with your right hand and call for bids.

If the audience is slow to start bidding, simply start things off yourself by pretending that someone has made a bid. Look toward the rear of the room and say, "You, sir? Thank you. The gentleman bids a penny—one cent is bid. Do I hear two?"

Bring your left hand up in front of you as you naturally would to write on the card, so the backs of your fingers are toward the audience. With the pencil in your right hand scribble "1¢" somewhere on the card. It makes no difference where since what you write on the card will never be shown. As you get bids of two cents and then three, jot down those numbers.

There is plenty of time as the bidding goes along to adjust the card and tag. You can turn your hand a little or move the card up or down with your other hand, as if to position it better for writing the bids. Part of the letters of the word "EXACTLY" will be visible through the hole in the card so you can make sure that is at the top.

When you have raised the bidding as high as it will go, say: "I have sixteen cents then" (or whatever the amount may be). ". . . Is that all? Going once, going twice—gone for sixteen cents!" Quickly write down the amount, but this time write through the hole in the card to print on the face of the tag. When you have finished writing it, keep the pencil in your right hand and tuck it into your outer breast pocket to leave it there; then let your left hand, holding the card and tag, drop to your side.

Look out at the audience and shake your head as if you were disappointed by the low bidding. Bring your left hand up and stare down at the card. "*Sixteen cents?* Sorry—but I just won't sell it to you for that." With your right hand crumple up the card and lift it away in that hand as you again drop your left hand to your side.

To the HIGHEST BIDDER

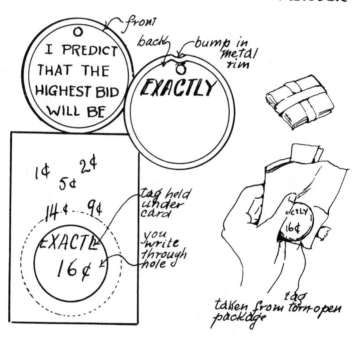

The tag remains in your left hand, loosely held there by the curl of your fingers and concealed by the back of your hand, which naturally falls into that position at your side. Don't make any attempt to "palm" the tag or to do anything tricky with it. Pay no attention to that hand at all.

Look at the crumpled card in your right hand, shake your head again, and say, "I refuse to accept your bid!" Crush the card and put it into the right-hand pocket of your jacket. Then smile and explain: "I won't accept your bid because if I took your money—I'd be cheating you. Instead, I'll give you what's inside the package absolutely free."

Pick up the package with your right hand and show it. Bring your left hand up in front of you and put the package into that hand right on top of the concealed tag. With your right hand tear open the tissue paper, spreading it wide. There is enough of the paper so it will pretty well cover your left hand, which now can be shown quite freely as you continue to tear the package open.

Just tear through the bottom of the paper. Pull the tag out through it a little. Turn your left hand to let the audience see the tag against the torn paper. Take the edge of the tag with your right thumb and first finger, slowly draw it the rest of the way out of the paper, and hold it up high. Crumple the paper in your left hand and toss it aside.

Hold your right hand with the tag above your head as you go to the spectator who made the last bid. Ask the person to read aloud what you wrote on the tag "hours ago." Glance at the tag to make sure you hold it so he will begin reading from the side that starts with the words, I PREDICT THAT . . .

As he finishes reading that side aloud, turn it over and give him the tag to read the other side, which completes your prediction that the highest bid would be . . . EXACTLY 16¢.

Weather Forecast

How it looks:

"One thing everybody tries to predict is the weather," you say, as you hold up a large card and read aloud the weather conditions printed on it in red. "Warmer, colder, cloudy, stormy, fair."

Turning to one of the spectators, you invite him to try to predict what tomorrow's weather will be. "Just make a guess. But don't tell us yet what it is. Look over this list of possibilities and decide in your own mind what kind of a day you think tomorrow will be. Let's see if I can pick up your mental forecast."

When he says he is thinking of one of the listed weather conditions, you turn the card so it faces you. "I'll make a little circle and put an X in it." Taking a black pen from your pocket, you mark the card without showing it to the audience. "All right. I've marked what I believe your forecast will be. . . . You can tell us now. What's your guess—warmer, colder, cloudy, stormy or fair?"

He calls out his mental choice, perhaps, "Stormy." You show the audience the card. The word you have marked with an X is STORMY.

"You were very positive about that, sir," you say. "I got the thought clearly. If you're as good at predicting the weather as you are at projecting your thoughts, we'd better expect a stormy day tomorrow."

What you need:

A 7-by-11-inch sheet of white poster board.

A red marking pen.

A broad-tipped black marking pen that can be clipped into your pocket.

A package of white, round, self-sticking "removable" labels, 1 inch in diameter. These are available at stationery stores, sold under various trade names such as Pres-a-ply.

A pair of scissors.

The secret and setup:

You only pretend to mark the card. The circle and X mark are drawn ahead of time on one of the labels. This is hidden, in a way that will be explained, so that your thumb secretly rolls the label into place and sticks it on the card after the spectator has called out what he is thinking. It looks as if you had marked the card itself, right opposite the word he had in mind.

The list of weather conditions should be printed so as to leave a wide margin at the left of the words. Start with the large card on a table, narrow edges top and bottom. With the red marking pen print WARMER in letters about 1 inch high, beginning about 2 inches down from the top and the same distance in from the left. Print each of the other weather conditions directly beneath the one above, with a good space between them. Turn the card with the printing face down and put it aside for a moment.

Take one of the self-sticking white labels and with the

scissors trim a tiny edge off the top and one side so it is no longer a perfectly round circle. This is done to give the label a slightly irregular shape, such as you would make if you quickly drew a circle with a pen. With the *black* pen draw a circle on the label, all the way around just inside the edge of it. Then mark a large *X* in the center.

Stick the *left half* of the label firmly to the *back* of the large card, about 1 inch down from the top left corner, but leave the right half of the label unstuck. Bend that free right-hand edge leftward and crease it slightly at the center of the label, so that right edge of it remains unstuck to the card and retains an inward curl. (If it later accidentally does become stuck flat, you can easily peel it free with a lift of your thumbnail.)

Have the card faceup on the table and clip the black pen into the outside breast pocket of your jacket.

What you do:

Pick up the card and hold it at the sides between both hands to show the audience what is printed on it. Your left hand is at the top left side of the card and your right hand at the lower right side of it, and the fingers of both hands are at the front and thumbs at the back. The ball of your left thumb should be touching the label that is hidden on the back of the card.

Read the printed list of weather conditions aloud and invite one of the spectators to try to predict what tomorrow's weather will be. "Just make a guess. But don't tell us yet what it is," you say. "Look over the list and decide in your own mind. . . . Let's see if I can pick up your mental forecast."

While you are talking, secretly press the ball of your left

thumb against the free edge of the label so that the label sticks to your thumb. Roll your thumb to the left and the label will peel off and remain attached to your thumb. The patter allows time to do this slowly, and the slight movement of your thumb is concealed by the card and by your fingers at the front.

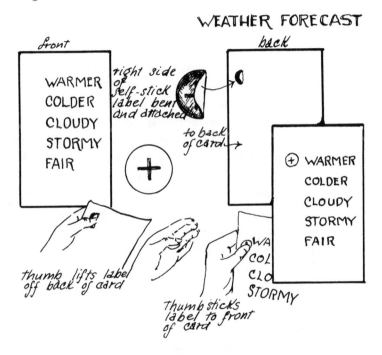

When the spectator says he is thinking of one of the weather conditions, draw your left thumb, the label stuck to it, in toward the palm of that hand. Keep the hand held up as it is. With your right hand turn the card around so it is facing you and grasp the top of the card again with the left hand.

Hold the card up with that hand and drop your right hand to your side. This is the natural way you would turn the card around, and it should look like nothing more than that.

Keep the card facing you, held by your left hand. The fingers are at the front of it and thumb behind, the label still stuck to your thumb. Bring your right hand over to your breast pocket and remove the pen. Move the pen up and down the list behind the card as if debating which word to mark. Scratch your fingernail on the card as you pretend to make a circle and put an X in it without actually marking the card. Put the pen away in your breast pocket again.

Now take the card with your right hand and drop your left arm to your side, keeping that thumb and the label that is attached to it hidden by your fingers. "All right. I've marked what I believe your forecast will be," you say to the spectator. "You can tell us now. What's your guess — warmer, colder, cloudy, stormy or fair?"

When he calls out his mental choice, bring your left hand up to the side of the card again so that your thumb goes behind the card *directly opposite the word he has chosen* and your fingers are at the front. Hold the card, still facing you, between both hands. Secretly roll your thumb to the right, catching the edge of the label against the card. This will peel the label off your thumb and stick it to the card. Smooth the label with your thumb and press it firmly into place.

You can look down at the card as you do this, as if checking the prediction. Take your time and transfer the label properly. Finally turn the card so the audience can see what appears to be the circle and X mark in front of the chosen word.